MALHAMDALE

Paul Hannon

HILLSIDE

HILLSIDE GUIDES - ACROSS THE NORTH

• •

Long Distance Walks

THE COAST TO COAST WALK   **FURNESS WAY**
DALES WAY COMPANION   **CLEVELAND WAY COMPANION**
THE WESTMORLAND WAY   **THE CUMBERLAND WAY**
NORTH BOWLAND TRAVERSE (David Johnson)
LADY ANNE'S WAY (Sheila Gordon)

Circular Walks - Lancashire
BOWLAND   **PENDLE & THE RIBBLE**

Circular Walks - Yorkshire Dales
THREE PEAKS COUNTRY
WALKS IN WHARFEDALE   **WALKS IN WENSLEYDALE**
WALKS ON THE HOWGILL FELLS
NIDDERDALE   **MALHAMDALE**   **SWALEDALE**

Circular Walks - North York Moors
BOOK ONE - WESTERN MOORS   **BOOK THREE - NORTHERN MOORS**
BOOK TWO - SOUTHERN MOORS

Circular Walks - South Pennines
WALKS IN BRONTE COUNTRY   **WALKS IN CALDERDALE**
ILKLEY MOOR

Circular Walks - North Pennines
TEESDALE

Hillwalking - Lake District
OVER LAKELAND MOUNTAINS   **OVER LAKELAND FELLS**

Pub Walks (Valerie Yewdall)
HARROGATE/WHARFE VALLEY   **HAWORTH/AIRE VALLEY**

Large format colour hardback
FREEDOM OF THE DALES

BIKING COUNTRY (Richard Peace)
YORKSHIRE DALES CYCLE WAY   WEST YORKSHIRE CYCLE WAY

80 DALES WALKS - an omnibus *(published by Cordee, Leicester)*

WALKING COUNTRY TRIVIA QUIZ
Over 1000 questions on the great outdoors

WALKING COUNTRY

MALHAMDALE

Paul Hannon

HILLSIDE

HILLSIDE
PUBLICATIONS
11 Nessfield Grove
Keighley
West Yorkshire
BD22 6NU

First published in 1986 in different format
as *Walks in the Craven Dales*.
This fully revised and extended edition
first published1995

© Paul Hannon 1986,1995

ISBN 1 870141 29 6

Cover illustration: Malham Cove
Back cover:
Gordale Scar; Malham Tarn
Gargrave; Rylstone Fell
(Paul Hannon/Big Country Picture Library)

Page 1:Rylstone Cross
Page 3: Leeds-Liverpool Canal

Printed in Great Britain by
Fretwell Print And Design
Goulbourne Street
Keighley
West Yorkshire

CONTENTS

INTRODUCTION

Malhamdale is the southernmost valley of the Yorkshire Dales National Park, and takes its name from the famous village for which all visitors make. Its river is the Aire, one of the major rivers of Yorkshire. Unlike its neighbours which also rise high on the hills of the Dales, the Aire has but a brief existence in these tranquil pastures before heading into the heart of industrial Yorkshire. Fortunately its time inside the Dales is well spent, and along with its numerous tributary becks it presents a highly compact area to which this guidebook is dedicated.

Not only is this a compact region, it offers rich contrasts. The western half needs little introduction, for the Malham district is renowned for its stunningly impressive scenery, with Malham Cove and Gordale Scar the jewels in the crown. The uplands above these major features contain a wealth of limestone delights, with Malham Tarn in the heart of things. Downstream from Malham the valley becomes immediately pastoral, with several villages nestling along the river down to Gargrave.

East of the Aire, the surroundings undergo a dramatic change. Here is typical gritstone country, with rocky outcrops, bracken covered slopes and some splendid heather moorland. The various becks flowing off the moors all meet the Aire by Skipton, some having emerged from attractive reservoirs.

The boundaries of this book are defined by the watersheds with the Ribble, Skirfare and Wharfe to the west, north and east respectively (though we do on occasions creep over them) and the limits of the National Park boundary to the south. Standing at this boundary is the fascinating market town of Skipton, an ideal base for the area: Walk 19 looks at it in detail.

On Cracoe Fell

In the very east of the area rises Barden Moor, highly valued grouse shooting country which has long been the subject of a negotiated access agreement with the landowner (the Duke of Devonshire's estates). Walkers are free to roam over the upland areas subject to certain restrictions, and Walks 20, 21 and 22 take advantage of this facility. The main point is that the moors can be 'closed' on certain days when shooting takes place (though not Sundays) and also at times of high fire risk. Notices are posted at all the access points, though disappointment can be avoided by ringing the estate office or a National Park Centre beforehand. Also worth knowing in advance is the fact that dogs are not allowed, other than on the rights of way.

Malham itself has an appeal very different to that of most Dales villages, in that the *majority* of its visitors come to walk, even though for most it's simply a return trip to the Cove. The village itself does however have much of interest, both old and new. A good number of cottages date from the 17th and early 18th centuries, and form several attractive groups. The impressive Listers Arms dates from 1723, and bears the arms of the Lords Ribblesdale, who built Malham Tarn House. In monastic times land hereabouts was shared between Bolton Priory and Fountains Abbey, and reminders of their granges are found in the naming of two of the numerous bridges over Malham Beck which divides the village. Monk Bridge was once a packhorse bridge, now widened to a road bridge, while Prior Moon's Bridge is highest of several clapper-bridges. Two modern, purpose-built structures are the youth hostel and the National Park Centre.

The Aire at Newfield Bridge, near Airton

Getting around

Public transport to the area is good, with Skipton very much the focal point. Buses from Keighley, Bradford, Leeds and Colne are the main routes in, while Skipton's railway station is well served on the Airedale line from Leeds and Bradford. North of Skipton there are also useful stations at Gargrave, Hellifield, Long Preston and Settle. Within the area, bus services run to Settle, Grassington, Embsay and Malham: the latter service, now much reduced, is operated by the locally famous Pennine buses from Gargrave. There is also a Skipton-Malham postbus, which serves many small villages en route. While only one of the 22 walks is described as a linear ramble, any number of permutations can be created by linking different sections, particularly using the bus. A brief comment on the availability of public transport is given at the start of each walk, though one really must consult a timetable to get up-to-date information.

Using the guide

Each walk is self-contained, with essential information being followed by a simple map and concise description of the route. Dovetailed between the bold print of the main route details are useful notes of features along the way, and interspersed are illustrations which both capture the flavour of the walks and document the many items of interest.

The sketch maps identify the location of the routes rather than the fine detail, and whilst the route description should be sufficient to guide one around, an Ordnance Survey map is recommended. The route as depicted can easily be plotted on the relevant OS map: all the walks are found on Landranger sheets 98 Wensleydale & Upper Wharfedale and 103 Blackburn & Burnley.

To gain the most from a walk, however, the remarkable detail of the 1:25,000 scale maps cannot be matched: they also serve to vary walks as desired, giving an improved picture of one's surroundings and the availability of linking paths. From the 1995 edition, **Outdoor Leisure 10 - Yorkshire Dales South** covers every walk in the book, and is therefore the perfect companion to the guide (earlier editions only missed part of Walk 18). Pathfinder 661 Skipton & Hellifield is an alternative map for the following walks: 8; 9; 11; 17; 18; 19; 20.

WALKING COUNTRY - MALHAMDALE

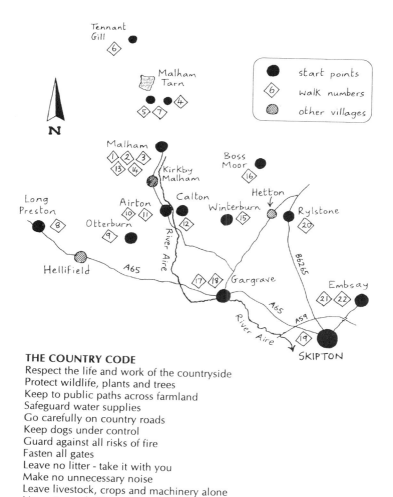

THE COUNTRY CODE
Respect the life and work of the countryside
Protect wildlife, plants and trees
Keep to public paths across farmland
Safeguard water supplies
Go carefully on country roads
Keep dogs under control
Guard against all risks of fire
Fasten all gates
Leave no litter - take it with you
Make no unnecessary noise
Leave livestock, crops and machinery alone
Use gates and stiles to cross fences, hedges and walls

MALHAM CLASSIC

START Malham   Grid ref. SD 900626

DISTANCE 4½ miles

ORDNANCE SURVEY MAPS
1:50,000
Landranger 98 - Wensleydale & Upper Wharfedale
1:25,000
Outdoor Leisure 10 - Yorkshire Dales South

ACCESS Start from the village centre. There is a large car park at the entrance to the village. Served by bus from Skipton.

☐ *From the car park head into the village, crossing the beck either by a footbridge by the forge, or by the road bridge and doubling back to follow the beck downstream. The short lane ends at a gate from where a broad path heads across the fields. At a double kissing-gate the path swings left to a barn, crosses to the left of the wall and continues in the same direction.* The outer portals of Gordale await, but as yet reveal nothing of the grandeur to come: Malham Cove, however, shows itself off back over the village.

Very soon Gordale Beck is joined and followed upstream. On entering a delightful section of woodland, the charming waterfall of Janet's Foss will be reached all too soon. Legend has it that Janet, local fairy queen, had a cave behind the falls. What is more certain is that this wood provides a rich habitat for a wide variety of flora and fauna: an information board is provided. **Here the path breaks off left to emerge onto the road to Gordale. Turn right along it for a short distance, crossing the beck (by the old bridge if you wish) and arriving at a gate on the left just before Gordale House. A well trodden path heads across the pasture to the unmistakable cliffs of Gordale Scar, which converge as we enter the dark confines.** For more on Gordale Scar please refer to WALK 14, which continues through the ravine.

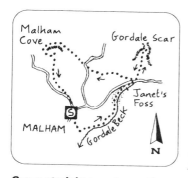

Our way now returns to the old bridge, where leave the road by a kissing-gate. From the wall corner just above, climb the field-side to a ladder-stile, then rise again to a gate at the top corner. Here a firm path runs along to the left, remaining with the wall beneath more open limestone country. At the end it slants up to the right to parallel the moor road to Malham Tarn, before joining it at a stile.

Cross straight over to another, and head away on a landrover track across the pasture. A wall is joined and followed as far as the next corner. When the wall turns away, there is a fork in the route. While the right branch rises up to a stile in the wall ahead, our way bears gently down to the left, with the limestone pavement atop Malham Cove revealed immediately below us. Drop down to a stile and gateway to gain access to the top of the Cove. Up to the right, the Dry Valley strikes away into the hills (see WALK 3). The extensive pavement atop the Cove is absolutely fascinating to tread, but with great care as the grikes in between have leg-damaging capabilities. The limestone cliff of Malham Cove rises 300ft from the valley: the waterfall that fell here must have been awesome!

At the far end, stiles send a stepped path descending the slopes at the end of the Cove. At the bottom, one can first bear left to access the very base of the mighty cliff. Issuing from the base is Malham Beck, the water having sunk on the moor. To return to the village, simply turn downstream with the beck, a broad man-made path returning through the fields to emerge onto the road just short of the village.

Malham Cove

11

PIKEDAW

START Malham   Grid ref. SD 900626

DISTANCE 5½ miles

ORDNANCE SURVEY MAPS
1:50,000
Landranger 98 - Wensleydale & Upper Wharfedale
1:25,000
Outdoor Leisure 10 - Yorkshire Dales South

ACCESS Start from the village centre. There is a large car park by the National Park Centre. Served by bus from Skipton.

☐ *From the car park entrance do not join the road into the village, but turn up the walled track on the right, then right again almost immediately on a similar track. Ignore the first branch left (opposite a barn) and carry on to take the next track climbing to the left. On levelling out it forks, and our way lies to the left, with Kirkby Fell and Pikedaw Hill rising steeply ahead. At the fourth barn on the left leave the track by a stile on the right, and head across the field to a prominent barn. From the stile by it head up the field, keeping above the beck to reach a stile at the top.*

Note the line of the Mid-Craven Fault along the course of the beck. The hills ahead also emphasise the marked transition from gritstone to limestone, as Kirkby Fell exhibits the former and Pikedaw the latter. Once height has been gained on leaving Malham, look back over the village to see, to particularly good advantage, the lynchets across the hillside. These are the ancient cultivation terraces of Anglian farmers, providing level strips to produce crops on steep slopes. **Above the stile continue on the same line, crossing the tiny beck where a broken wall comes in on the right. A sketchy path materialises and stays fairly close to the beck to arrive at a stile in the wall ahead.**

From here a detour to the top of Pikedaw Hill can be made by a short steep pull up to the right, the top being crowned by a substantial cairn. Pikedaw is probably the best viewpoint in this book, in terms of appreciating the countryside dealt with in this guide. Though blocked by higher fells westward, the eastern sector of the view is ample compensation. Pikedaw is best known, however, for its early 19th century mining activity. The chief target was calamine, a zinc ore, and evidence of this industry abounds in the form of shafts, levels and spoil-heaps. Steps must be retraced to the stile to resume the walk, which involves a loss of height to which there is no alternative.

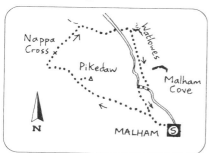

From the stile head straight up the slope in front, passing by a marker-post confirming the way. At the top of a steep climb the gradient eases at an interesting-looking cave, and the path, now clearer, heads away in the same direction. Swinging round to the right, the path makes its way across a limestone pavement to meet a wider path at a signpost. On arrival, note a brief glimpse of the crouching lion of Penyghent through the gap ahead. It appears again on the descent from Nappa Cross. **Head to the left to climb gently to Nappa Gate, passing an old calamine shaft on the way. The gate marks the high point of the walk.**

After the gate leave the path and turn right on a lesser one, passing Nappa Cross. Nappa Cross is one of several wayside crosses in the area, a guidepost for travellers since monastic times. Set into the wall, the restored shaft stands in its original base. **Beyond the cross, slope across to a gate. Two further gates are encountered as the path makes its way down the fell, soon reaching a gate in a corner, and then descending a pasture to meet the lane out of the village at Langscar**

Nappa Cross, looking to Malham Tarn

Gate. Cross straight over to another gate and head down the field: when a stile appears in front, turn sharp right to reach a prominent stile in the wall there. The path, though sketchy, is reasonably easy to follow as it runs roughly parallel with the road up to the right.

The cairn on Pikedaw

After crossing an intervening collapsed wall, two further ones are crossed by stiles, from where an improved path leads to two more in very quick succession. Malham Cove is now just across to the left, but our way continues, sketchily again, to two more neighbouring stiles, the latter returning us onto the lane. Turn uphill for a short distance to a sharp bend, and here take a gate on the left: a track heads down to a gate where it becomes enclosed by walls to lead in pleasant fashion back past an earlier junction and down to a T-junction. To include the village at the finish, turn left here and almost immediately right to emerge opposite Beck Hall. A right turn will lead back to the car park.

Monk Bridge, Malham

ABOVE MALHAM COVE

START Malham   Grid ref. SD 900626

DISTANCE 5 miles

ORDNANCE SURVEY MAPS
1:50,000
Landranger 98 - Wensleydale & Upper Wharfedale
1:25,000
Outdoor Leisure 10 - Yorkshire Dales South

ACCESS Start from the village centre. There is a large car park at the entrance to the village. Served by bus from Skipton.

A very easy walk through stunning limestone scenery: a must!

☐ *From the car park pass through the village, keeping left at the junction by the bridge. After the cluster of buildings at Town Head the lane begins to climb: we soon leave it by a gate signposted on the right, with the majestic Cove already in full view directly ahead.* The popularity of the approach to Malham Cove is evidenced by the state of the main path, on which admirable strengthening work has been carried out to cope with the incredible numbers of visitors. Unfortunately, but necessarily, the climb up the side is now on a man-made stairway. A selfish thought maybe, but why couldn't this natural gem be half a dozen miles from the nearest road?

A path leads to the very foot of the cliffs. The great limestone wall of Malham Cove rises 300 feet from the valley floor: it is difficult to imagine the waterfall that once plunged over the cliff. Issuing from the base is Malham Beck, the water having sunk on the moor. *To progress further, retrace steps a little to climb the man-made steps round the left side of the Cove. A stile at the top leads to the extensive limestone pavement covering the Cove-top.* Though fascinating to tread, great care must be taken on crossing it, for the grikes in between have great leg-damaging capabilities.

Having reached the end of the pavement at the centre of the Cove top a wall is met. Ignore both the stile and the gate however, and follow our side of the wall away from the Cove. After a stile in an intervening wall the crags on either side close in as we proceed along the floor of Watlowes, the Dry Valley. Comb Hill and Dean Moor Hill form the impressive twin portals at its head. These lofty cliffs - really 'ladders' of small crags - beckon one along Watlowes' deep rugged confines. With this at one end and the top of the Cove at the other, Watlowes is some little valley!

At the dramatic valley-head the path escapes by climbing to a stile in front, from where swing sharp right with a fence to round a ledge under Dean Moor Hill. An 80ft waterfall once plunged over the cliffs here. *Soon the outcrops are left behind and a wall provides company across the open moor to lead unerringly to Water Sinks.*

At Water Sinks the outflow from Malham Tarn, which for its brief existence is known as Malham Water, disappears deep into the ground. It does not return to the surface again for more than two miles, finally appearing at Aire Head Springs (see WALK 13). A commonly held misconception was that it re-appeared at the base of the Cove, but chemical tests long since disproved this theory: just one of the many wonders of this limestone district! Also on arrival at Water Sinks, Malham Tarn House comes into view (but not the tarn itself).

A line of telegraph poles indicate the proximity of the road across the moor, and it is soon reached at a gate by following the beck upstream. From the open road across the moor, the walk could be extended to incorporate the tarn (see WALK 5). *Turn right through the gate on the road: this is Water Sinks Gate. Leave at once by a faint path on the right, which crosses the pasture slanting gently up to eventually arrive at a wall-stile. Here we pick up the Pennine Way, and now make use of it to return to the Cove. Over the stile we enter the extensive sheep pasture of Prior Rakes, passing some pools.* These are former dewponds, created by the monks to help slake their cattle's thirst: this route leading to Trougate was in fact used in monastic times. **Head on to the next wall to enter and pass through the well defined trench of Trougate between low limestone outcrops. Past further intervening walls another path is met. Follow this back down to the right to return to the wall at the top of Malham Cove.**

Malham Cove

Re-cross the limestone pavement and return to the foot of the Cove. Use the path back to Malham as far as the first gate, and then cross the beck by means of a footbridge of stone slabs. Turn right up the slope, and a faint path rises towards the first of three stiles in cross-walls. Continue on to a gap in a collapsing wall, and then follow the wall to the right to reach a stile. The collapsed walls hereabouts are the remains of Iron age field boundaries, and must be left alone. **After a few enclosed yards, head away in the same direction with a wall now on the left. On reaching a small shelter, the way becomes enclosed again, and remains so to re-enter Malham in fine style. Debouching onto a back lane, continue straight down past the youth hostel into the village centre.**

Water Sinks

17

LITTONDALE

START Street Gate   Grid ref. SD 904656

DISTANCE 12 miles

ORDNANCE SURVEY MAPS
1:50,000
Landranger 98 - Wensleydale & Upper Wharfedale
1:25,000
Outdoor Leisure 10 - Yorkshire Dales South

ACCESS Street Gate is the point where Mastiles Lane branches off the Malham-Malham Tarn road (the road east of the Cove). There is ample verge parking at the junction.

This walk to the inspiring objective of lovely Littondale offers exceptionally easy walking on cushioned green ways.

☐ *From the crossroads of ways forsake the tarmac and head north along the unsurfaced drive heading for Malham Tarn. Beyond a gate it enters the environs of Malham Tarn itself, running near the shore and approaching the wooded grounds of the house.*

At 1230 feet above sea-level, Malham Tarn is an extensive sheet of water: its existence in this limestone preserve is due to the layer of Silurian slate on which it stands. This snippet of geological knowledge is a rare survivor from many people's (including the author's) schooldays. With its surrounding wetlands, the tarn is home to a variety of birdlife. The surrounding calcareous grassland, woodland and limestone pavement further contribute to its status as a National Nature Reserve. It is jointly managed by its owners, the National Trust, and the Field Studies Council, who operate at Malham Tarn House. The monks of Fountains Abbey held fishing rights on the tarn, while Charles Kingsley drew his inspiration to create The Water Babies.

Follow the drive along the shore of the tarn, passing the cliffs of Great Close Scar. Do not enter the woods at the cattle-grid, but climb the slope to the right. *This affords an excellent retrospective view of the whole of the tarn.* A green path materialises to rise to the saddle between Highfolds (left) and Great Close Hill. Beyond the gap the path runs along towards Middle House Farm, but beyond an intervening fence slant steadily left, rising to meet a track climbing from the farm to a stile by a gate.

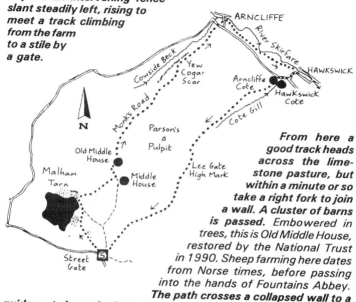

From here a good track heads across the limestone pasture, but within a minute or so take a right fork to join a wall. A cluster of barns is passed. *Embowered in trees, this is Old Middle House, restored by the National Trust in 1990. Sheep farming here dates from Norse times, before passing into the hands of Fountains Abbey.* The path crosses a collapsed wall to a guidepost: here the less obvious Darnbrook path (see WALK 5) goes off to the left. *The Monk's Road leaves no doubt as to its original patrons, followed by packhorses and now walkers, who are treated to ever expanding vistas over the scars to Littondale entrenched between Darnbrook and Birks Fells. In due course it will lead us to Arncliffe.*

Little further description is needed as the path runs on through outcrops, pavements and a miscellany of stiles. In time the path drops a little to run along the well-defined crest of Yew Cogar Scar. *Below, the idiosyncratic meanderings of Cowside Beck earned it limited fame when it provided the concluding shots for a long-running television farm serial.* As the scars recede the path gets to *grips with the descent to Arncliffe, clearly in view on the dale floor. A delightful little lane is joined to lead into the village, rather handily adjacent to the* Falcon *inn on the green.*

Arncliffe is one of the most attractive yet least spoilt villages in the Dales, and is regarded as the 'capital' of Littondale. A variety of characterful grey-stone houses stand back in relaxed manner from a spacious green. The unpretentious inn maintains this mood, and is in fact the only hostelry in the area to serve its ale in that unrivalled fashion, directly from the barrel. Across the shapely bridge, the house at Bridge End played host to Charles Kingsley during his Water Babies period.

From the green cross to the up-dale road, but leave it almost at once for a drive on the right immediately before the church. Out of sight of the green is St Oswald's church, which claims its own niche embowered in trees in a beautiful riverside setting. Though largely rebuilt last century, the solid tower dates back 500 years. Inside is a list of the Littondale men who marched off to fight at Flodden Field in 1513. **At the end of the drive is a barn, and to its right we emerge into a field. An uncomplicated stroll ensues, downstream with the Skirfare.** This relaxing 1½ miles are a lovely amble along the dale floor, which can positively abound in bird life. **The path is generally clear, and little description is needed other than keeping an eye on the map and the waymarks. Initially in the company of the river, the path keeps its distance for the middle section before rejoining its bank to reach Hawkswick footbridge.**

St. Oswald's, Arncliffe

Just across it is Hawkswick, last village in Littondale. Being the only one off the 'main' up-dale road, its cosy setting remains wonderfully undisturbed. In season, refreshments may be obtained.

Without crossing the bridge, turn up the short byway onto a lane. This narrowest of roads climbs up to the right to join the main Littondale road, which is followed a short distance to the right. The second of near parallel drives should be taken to rise to the farm at Arncliffe Cote. Arncliffe Cote was an outlier of the grange at Kilnsey belonging to the monks of Fountains Abbey: across the beck is Hawkswick Cote. Our green road over the hills towards Malham perhaps not surprisingly dates back the same 600 or so years. **A track takes over past the buildings to soon emerge onto the grassy fell.**

After a zigzag it commences a long, very gradual climb high above the ravine of Cote Gill across to the left. Though hardly demanding rest-stops, the climb by often-dry Cote Gill should be broken to enjoy increasing vistas back over Littondale. **The pastures are long and the going easy as the higher reaches of the gill and surrounding uplands are penetrated on a resplendent track on velvet turf. A hint of steepness is encountered before a brief foray with real 'fell-like' terrain on the highest point, Lee Gate High Mark.**

The summit of the walk reveals a sweeping prospect over Craven to that great landmark Pendle Hill, in Lancashire. **The track winds down through the extensive pasture of Great Close.** Great Close was the setting, 200 years ago, for the biggest cattle fairs in the north. **In the very corner an exuberant stream is forded and a final pasture crossed to meet Mastiles Lane at Street Gate.**

Old Cote Moor and Great Whernside from Cote Gill

5

DARNBROOK

START Water Sinks Gate   Grid ref. SD 893657

DISTANCE 8 miles

ORDNANCE SURVEY MAPS
1:50,000
Landranger 98 - Wensleydale & Upper Wharfedale
1:25,000
Outdoor Leisure 10 - Yorkshire Dales South

ACCESS Start from the roadside car park where the outflow from Malham Tarn meets the road.

☐ *From Water Sinks Gate follow the beck - **Malham Water** - upstream across the open moor for a two minute walk to the outflow of the tarn. Here are splendid views over the breezy sheet of water to Malham Tarn House, enveloped in trees beneath Highfolds Scar, and Fountains Fell along to the left.*

At 1230 feet above sea-level, Malham Tarn is an extensive sheet of water: its existence in this limestone preserve is due to the layer of Silurian slate on which it stands. This snippet of geological knowledge is one of the few survivors from many people's (including the author's) schooldays. With its surrounding wetlands, the tarn is home to a variety of birdlife. The surrounding calcareous grassland, woodland and limestone pavement further contribute to its status as a National Nature Reserve. It is jointly managed by its owners, the National Trust, and the Field Studies Council, who operate at Tarn House. The monks of Fountains Abbey held fishing rights on the tarn, while Charles Kingsley drew inspiration to create The Water Babies.

Turn right along the shore to the top end of a walled plantation, and go left on a broad, green way to merge with the main drive at a gate.

Follow the drive along the shore of the tarn, passing the cliffs of Great Close Scar. Do not enter the woods at the cattle-grid, but climb the slope to the right. This affords excellent retrospective view of the whole of the tarn. *A green path materialises to rise to the saddle between Highfolds (left) and Great Close Hill.* This is the Monk's Road, which leaves no doubt as to its original patrons: walkers now stride where packhorses toiled.

Beyond the gap, the path runs along towards Middle House Farm, but beyond an intervening fence slant steadily left, rising to meet a track climbing from the farm to a stile by a gate. From here a good track heads across the limestone pasture, but within a minute or so take a right fork to join a wall. A cluster of barns is passed. Embowered in trees, this is Old Middle House, restored in 1990 by the National Trust. Sheep farming here dates from Norse times, before passing into the hands of Fountains Abbey. *The path crosses a collapsed wall to a guidepost: here we leave the Arncliffe path and take the sketchier left fork. It contours round the slopes of these wonderful limestone uplands, with a wall coming in on the right.* Ahead we are treated to grand views over to Darnbrook Fell, with its 'boss' Fountains Fell entering the scene on the left.

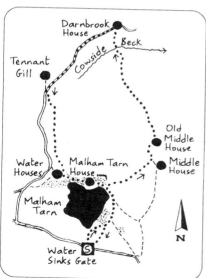

A stile crosses the wall, from where the path heads off through more outcrops. Strongly evident on the brow are the pronounced wall patterns of an ancient British settlement. *At this point the path almost completely fades. Follow the line of rocks downhill, with the farm at Darnbrook soon appearing ahead. As the wall below appears, look for a cairn just across to the right, worth a modest detour.* It serves to mark a fine viewpoint down Cowside Beck to the floor of Littondale, backed by the two tiers of Old Cote Moor and, behind that, Buckden Pike.

Aiming for the farm, descend to a gateway in the wall. Bear down to the right of the dry side-valley below, and from the remnants of a wall a green way slants down to a stone slab bridge over Cowside Beck. From the stile by the beck head for a gap by the barn in front, and continue across the fields by a further stile and out by a barn onto the road at Darnbrook. Darnbrook House is an isolated and historic farmstead, dating back over 600 years when it had connections with Fountains Abbey. The present building has a 17th century datestone and mullioned windows.

Turn left along this narrow lane for 1¼ miles, a good deal of which can be trodden on open verges. At a sharp left turn just after the track to Tennant Gill Farm on the right, leave the road along a sketchy path across the open pasture on the left to drop down to a stile. Climb beyond it to a wall-corner then turn to accompany the wall across undulating pastures. After a stile in a cross-wall continue alongside the wall. En route, a clever little barn is passed, with three entrances each accessing different enclosures. *The next stile leads through a shallow limestone trough, emerging by way of a canopy of trees onto the drive at Water Houses.*

Turn left along this track through the wooded grounds of Malham Tarn House, passing between rock walls to reach the rear of the house. The impressive-looking Malham Tarn House was built as a shooting lodge for Lord Ribblesdale, and was much improved by the

The viewpoint cairn above Darnbrook, looking down Cowside Beck towards Arncliffe, backed by Birks Fell

24

Malham Tarn House

Morrison family in the 1850's. It is now well established in an ideal situation as a field studies centre. Just beyond it, note the high walls of Highfolds Scar projecting above the trees. **Continue out to the tarn shore which we left so long ago. Retrace steps to the gate at the entrance, and then bear right on the green pathway, past the plantation corner to cross the moor back to the starting point.** With luck, an ice cream van will be plying its trade.

Malham Tarn and Highfolds Scar

6

FOUNTAINS FELL

START Tennant Gill   Grid ref. SD 884691

DISTANCE 11½ miles

ORDNANCE SURVEY MAPS
1:50,000
Landranger 98 - Wensleydale & Upper Wharfedale
1:25,000
Outdoor Leisure 10 - Yorkshire Dales South

ACCESS Tennant Gill Farm is on the Malham-Arncliffe road. There is verge parking immediately before the drive to the farm. Please do not park beyond the cattle-grid, nor obstruct any access. An alternative start with better parking is mid-walk at Dale Head, on the Stainforth-Halton Gill road, though strictly speaking this isn't our area!

This lengthy circuit of one of Craven's bulky mountains affords excellent views of the Three Peaks, and takes the walker off the better known paths.

☐ **Head along the drive towards the farm.** *Above are limestone tors that will shortly give way to the upper gritstone reaches of Fountains Fell. Already we enjoy a sweeping view over Darnbrook and Cowside to Great Whernside.* **Without entering the yard turn left up the track, and level with the buildings take a gentler track up to the left to climb to a stile onto the open fell. Bear left away, but within two minutes leave the track as directed by way of a footpath climbing directly away, alongside the remnants of a wall. This smashing green pathway climbs for some time to reach a cairn.** *If not having looked back yet, do so now to espy Malham Tarn, with the miniature peaks of Flasby Fell behind.*

Just a little higher is a smaller cairn, and the path forsakes the old wall by turning sharply right. Now it contours for some time to arrive at a stile off the Malham Tarn estate. From this point the way,

entirely unmistakable, continues as an intermittent green way and hard, recently made track. Unfortunately the latter surface pre-dominates, and while this section did until recent times have its moister moments, some would say this equivalent to a bulldozed shooters' track is slightly over the top. Either way, as more height is gained the views extend, with underling Darnbrook Fell just in front decorated by curious boxed plantations, and a barrage of higher ground towards Wharfedale, with Great Whernside the dominant force.

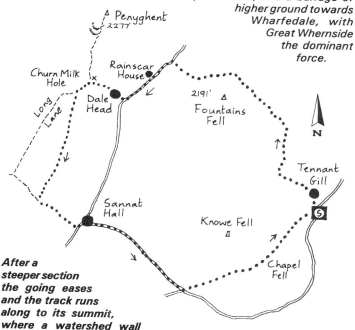

After a steeper section the going eases and the track runs along to its summit, where a watershed wall awaits. Probably the finest moment of the walk comes on approaching this point, as Penyghent, the 'Lion' of Ribblesdale, rears its head directly in front. It is ably supported by its two loftier brethren, Ingleborough and Whernside.

The actual summit of Fountains Fell will be seen just a few minutes across to the left, surmounted by a most solid pile of stones. Few will resist the call to claim a mountain top so accessible, but those venturing across should be aware it is off the public footpath, and be sure to resist peering down into the mineshafts that abound.

27

Two prominent shafts, both unsecurely fenced, are just off the main path: one on the left, at the start of the detour to the summit, and the other just before the stile in the summit wall. Children should not be allowed near them, they are *EXTREMELY DEEP*.

These upper reaches of Fountains Fell are dotted with various remains of the mining days, for both coal and lead were won here, and spoil heaps abound. The colliery was at its peak in the early 19th century, and our route of ascent has been along the old colliers' way. Two stone men stood just off the path over the top, but had sadly been torn down on my last visit. En route to the summit, a curious feature known as the 'Igloo' is passed. This stone hut is likely to have been erected by miners.

The all round panorama is quite magnificent: Whernside and Wild Boar Fell, incidentally, are visible from the path but hidden from the summit view. Major features, working clockwise, are as follows: Ingleborough, Penyghent, Whernside, Howgill Fells, Baugh Fell, Plover Hill, Wild Boar Fell, Cross Fell, Great Dun Fell, High Seat, Dodd Fell, Little Fell, Mickle Fell, Great Shunner Fell, Wether Fell, Lovely Seat, Rogan's Seat, Yockenthwaite Moor, Birks Fell, Buckden Pike, Little Whernside, Great Whernside, Meugher, Grassington Moor, Parson's Pulpit, Simon's Seat, Barden Moor, Skipton Moor, Rombalds Moor, Fountains Fell South Top, Grizedales, Rye Loaf Hill, Pendle Hill, Grindleton Fell, White Hill and the eastern Bowland fells, and Ward's Stone, highest point in Bowland.

Stone men (R.I.P.) on
Fountains Fell,
looking north-east

BUCKDEN PIKE 2303'
Darnbrook Fell 2047'
Birks Fell 1998'
Little Whernside 1985'
GREAT WHERNSIDE 2310'

Back at the stile, cross and head away, a more attractive track (another miners' way) winding along to an edge. Here Penyghent is revealed more fully - with a glimpse of Halton Gill at the head of Littondale. *The track slants down the fellside, initially beneath a craggy wall and then in super condition all the way down to meet a wall, continuing down with it to quickly reach a corner. Take the stile ahead to descend to the open moor road from Halton Gill.* Maps showing a direct footpath across the moor to cut a corner of the road are now out of date. Looking back, Fountains Fell at last cuts a reasonably rounded profile. *Go left along the road, passing Rainscar House to arrive at the drive to Dale Head.*

Here there are likely to be several parked cars, for this is the start of the shortest route up Penyghent, and the way by which our young 'uns first climbed the hill. *Cross the cattle-grid and then turn right along the short drive.* Dale Head Farm once served the packhorse trade. All the while, Penyghent grows in grandeur - surely we're going to climb it? *The trackway continues past the farm, rising only slightly and advancing nearer the mountain.* This will probably be the only time on the walk you encounter fellow walkers.

Passing a large crater on the left, the track reaches a fork. Just down to the right is the pothole of Churn Milk Hole, an impressive foreground to Penyghent as we do the unthinkable, and take our leave. On a good day, the energetic may fall for the detour to Penyghent: they could be gone an hour. *Turn left to leave the crowds behind, as our left branch runs on to a wall corner.* Here is the pair of old boundary stones depicted.

Boundary stones, Churn Milk Hole

The track (Long Lane) heads away with the wall, but before it reaches the corner of the enclosure, bear off to the left to a ladder-stile. From here a faint path heads away, still with the wall. Over to the right Ingleborough returns to view, as do the scars of Horton Quarry: indeed, at one point this and the two Helwith Bridge quarries *look almost ready to merge to form one continuous eyesore. As we are in effect on Penyghent's broad south ridge, keep looking back to see its increasing end-on aspect. Note also that older maps won't show our path, as it was only created in the 1980's.* **At the end of a second enclosure we are transferred to the other side of the wall, but the direction remains the same all the way.** *Just across to the left is a limestone pavement.*

On a more pronounced drop, with Settle conspicuous ahead at the foot of Ribblesdale, the thin path bears off left from the wall. At the bottom of the enclosure is Moor Head Lane, with a wall heading away from it as a target. The cart track is joined with a ladder-stile in front. Don't cross it, but turn left along the track. It quickly rises a short way to become enclosed, then winds along to meet the Stainforth-Halton Gill road again. *Over to our left, Fountains Fell takes on its more traditional undistinguished outline. Turn left the short way to a junction, then turn right here at Sannat Hall Farm.*

Here begins a rather prolonged road walk (1¾ miles), *not helped by the steep down and up to begin with. The re-ascent is enlivened by the re-appearance of Penyghent. The road offers some decent verges in its unenclosed section, and is at least a quiet country lane.* **The time to leave cannot be missed, for it coincides with the final disappearance of Penyghent, and the point of arriving at a junction with the Malham-Langcliffe road. A stile on the left sends us off back onto lovely cushioned turf.**

There is no visible path, but from the stile itself the next one can be discerned, high on the skyline to the right. Slant across to an old quarry, just past which a thin green trod forms to lead unerringly up to the stile. Maintain the same line beyond it, slanting up towards a prominent limestone scar on the skyline. The path becomes very faint part-way up, but returns near the scars to pass through a small dip to the left. Now swing round behind this limestone knoll, bearing right towards a curved wall corner. **Head away left with the wall (on the right) on a clearer track now.** *All this is grand - Malham Tarn is well seen in near entirety over to the right, with Fountains Fell, Darnbrook Fell and Great Whernside all on view.* **At a cairn on a brow, the path bears away from the wall, down to a waiting ladder-stile.**

Heading away from this, quickly keep straight ahead as the pathway curves around to the right, descending to another such stile. A once-enclosed way heads off with a wall, and from the gate at the end cross a pathless field with a shallow dry valley on the right. As the wall appears ahead, bear down to the left to locate a stile in a slight hollow. Above now are some fine limestone scars, above where we began, in fact. Head off again through a gateway in a fence just above a fence corner, and advance to the far corner of the field to a gate back onto the road where it all began.

Penyghent from Fountains Fell

STOCKDALE

START   Water Sinks Gate   Grid ref. SD 893657

DISTANCE 9 miles

ORDNANCE SURVEY MAPS
1:50,000
Landranger 98 - Wensleydale & Upper Wharfedale
1:25,000
Outdoor Leisure 10 - Yorkshire Dales South

ACCESS Start from the roadside car park where the outflow
from Malham Tarn meets the road.

*This high level march takes us into the territory of Ribblesdale
without the effort of descending into it: largely crowd-free!*

☐ **Leave the car park by taking the gate over Malham Water
emerging from the unseen tarn, and head along the road verge for
the best part of a mile.** *On the left is a smelt mill chimney restored
by Earby Mines Research Group in the 1970's.* **At the junction with
the Malham-Langcliffe road, take the gate on the left, just across.
Bear half-right to a stile out of the fenced enclosure, and continue
slanting over the pasture, aiming up to a junction of walls in various
stages of collapse. A thin way can be discerned here.**

**Head away to the right with the wall from the stile, (pecks on the
OS map exaggerate the state of these walls) then on through a
collapsed wall near a junction, and over a brow to find a stile and
gate in the wall ahead. On a thin path now through a slightly moist
big pasture.**

*Things perk up with Ingleborough, Queen of Yorkshire's mountains
seen ahead. Whernside's whaleback appears to its right, with, on
a clear day, Black Combe almost 50 miles distant on the horizon.*

32

And then, like a ghost ship silently floating into harbour, mighty Penyghent moves in. From the moment of its first appearance until its disappearance, Penyghent rules the roost. This Pennine moorland scene is now far removed from Malham's orderliness, a stark contrast indeed. **The green way of the Gorbeck road is joined and a very pleasant, clear track ensues. A couple more walls are passed through before crossing towards the right-hand wall which is then followed.** *The mountain panorama now includes Ingleborough, Great Coum, Whernside, the dome of Yarlside popping up from the Howgill Fells, Baugh Fell, Penyghent, Plover Hill and Fountains Fell.*

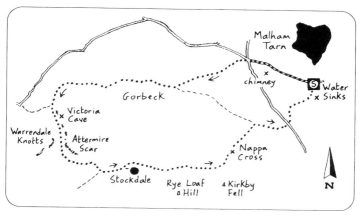

Glorious strides lead on, then out of the blue a stony track comes in. *On a clear day the distant prospect of Caw and the Coniston Fells is revealed to the left of Ingleborough.* **The old road winds down** *- ahead are the rounded swellings of the Bowland moors, then round the corner the Settle hills just ahead: Pendle Hill appears through a gap.* **Beyond a stile on the right, the track runs on to a gate. Don't go through it but take a stile on the left to run along the level to approach Victoria Cave, hidden up to the left.**

The cave is very definitely not hidden when you get up to it. The massive entrance has been blasted to this size in modern times, but the cave's history goes back through countless periods. It has yielded evidence of a richly varied occupancy, including bones of rhinoceros, hippopotamus, bear and mammoth, and also Stone age man.

Victoria Cave

From the enormous entrance a path returns to the main one to resume the walk, soon running on through an open pasture with the contorted tors of Warrendale Knotts on the right. The path drops to a gateway beneath the impressive Attermire Scar. Strictly speaking, the right of way goes through the wall to join the path alongside the wall behind, thence turns left and back through the aforementioned gateway beneath Attermire. The land on the Attermire side of the wall is, however, currently open to visitors under the Countryside Stewardship scheme.

Retiring Attermire Cave is to be found within the scar, a dark slit located high up the limestone cliff: with a sense of adventure and a reliable torch (and some common sense!) it can be penetrated a fair way in by mere mortals. **Here the main path heads off right through the gateway, bound for Settle. Less obvious is our route, which follows a very sketchy way contouring around to the left beneath Attermire Scar. The way is clearly marked as it rises gently through several pastures - gates all the way - to emerge onto surfaced Stockdale Lane: go left.** *Enjoy now views across this secluded side valley dominated by the hugely prominent Rye Loaf Hill.*

This is classic Craven Fault country - millstone grit to the right, with us still very much amid limestone. **Don't take the road down to Stockdale Farm, but use a gate on the left as a track continues above the wall.** *Note the farm's isolation: though in truth no distance from Settle, it is the only settlement in its own valley.* **The track runs on and on, gently up to eventually reach its zenith.** *In*

*poor weather keep right on the top when the path is unclear -
remember there's a wall on the right. **A level section ensues on top,
and a cairn is soon reached.** Although this is a pass, it is virtually
as high as the hills through which it runs! Revealed ahead is a
wonderful prospect of Malham Tarn and Moor, and more distantly
Buckden Pike and Great Whernside.*

**As Nappa Gate is reached the
old trackway commences its
descent. Don't go through, however, but turn left with the wall
on a thinner path. Nappa Cross
is quickly reached.** Nappa Cross
is one of several wayside crosses
in the area, a guidepost for
travellers since monastic times.
Set into the wall, the restored
shaft stands in its original base.

Jubilee Cave, looking out

**Beyond the cross, slope across
to a gate. Two further gates are
encountered as the path makes
its way down the fell, soon**
reaching a gate in a corner, and then descending a pasture, now
on the Gorbeck road again, to meet the lane out of the village at
Langscar Gate. Go left a few yards, then turn off the open road by
a track on the right. This broad grassy way crosses to a wall corner.
**From the gate head directly away to
the right, rising over Dean Moor to see
the starting point just ahead.** With
luck, an ice cream van will be plying its
trade.

*Smelt Mill Chimney,
Malham Moor*

8

LANGBER LANE

START Long Preston   Grid ref. SD 834582

DISTANCE   4½ miles

ORDNANCE SURVEY MAPS
1:50,000
Landranger 103 - Blackburn & Burnley
1:25,000
Outdoor Leisure 10 - Yorkshire Dales South *or*
Pathfinder 661 - Skipton & Hellifield

ACCESS Start from the village green outside the *Maypole Inn.* There is parking alongside the green and on the other side of the main road. Skipton-Settle buses pass through, and there is a station on the Leeds-Morecambe/Carlisle line.

Long Preston is well named: it is spread along the bustling A65 and looks forward to the day when its main street no longer quakes to the rumble of heavy traffic. It is in fact a very pleasant village that merits more than the second glance it rarely gets from those rushing through. Focal point is the green, graced by a maypole that is annually put to suitable use. Facing the green is the appropriately named inn, with another just along the street. There is also a Post office/store and a curiously located outdoor clothing shop.

Strictly speaking, as a Ribblesdale village, Long Preston is outwith the scope of this book. With partner Hellifield, however, it occupies something of a no-man's-land, and is invariably excluded from all thoughts of Ribblesdale, which generally end their interest at Settle. Downstream, the no-man's-land extends to the Lancashire border, Gisburn, and the true Ribble Valley. It had to find sanctuary somewhere, and the hinterland we are about to explore is firmly attached to the Malhamdale hills, indeed on Langber Lane we can nod at ramblers on WALK 9. What cold-shouldered Hellifield does not share with Long Preston, however, is National Park status.

❑ *From the green head away from the main road on School Lane. Bear right past the school, and just yards past the junction there a green lane heads off to the left. This cuts a corner of the road, but misses out the church. If visiting the church, remain on the* narrow lane. The church gate is to the right, just around the corner. St. Mary's church is rather tucked away, but worth a visit. Like its village, it too is long, with a heavy, low-slung roof. Its Norman font has a Jacobean cover, while in the churchyard, near the porch, is a 17th century dated sundial, also bearing many initials, and restored in 1980.

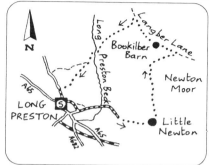

Leave along the church front to a little gate out of the churchyard back onto New House Lane. Already we have views over the Ribble Valley to the familiar landmark of Pendle Hill: it will remain in our sights for virtually all the walk. *Quickly picking up the direct green lane, continue on to the lane's demise at Little Newton. Keep left of the farm buildings to a set of pens. Here the path forks: take a gate on the left to join the bank of Newton Gill. Within yards a shapely bridge carries us over it and a clear grassy track accompanies it upstream. It fades at Waterfall Rock, where an exposed tilted rock strata overlooks a hollow above a minor waterfall. Just beyond, a stile admits to a corner of Newton Moor.*

Resume upstream, initially very pleasantly along the steep flank of the meandering beck. A higher level trod runs on from above the stile. As the slopes open out rise up a little, only a faintest of trod is traceable. Over to the left is a nice glimpse of Bowland, with Whelp Stone Crag prominent. *Curve around level ground above a confluence and wall corner, with the beck and parallel wall over to the left, to reach a junction with the wall ahead. Down to the left a stile and tiny footbridge are not seen until the very last moment. Go left up the wall-side to a stile on the brow then slant right up the vast reedy pasture to appproach a wall-corner on the left.* Ahead now to the east is a good prospect of the Crookrise edges on Barden Moor. *Ahead also, a ladder-stile onto Langber Lane beckons. Turn left along this old green way. It quickly reaches the house at Bookilber Barn, there becoming more solidly surfaced.*

It continues most amiably along past a couple of opportunities to return more directly to the village. Ahead, the flat top of Ingleborough is briefly revealed, while over to the left is a vast sweep featuring the South Pennines, Weets Hill, Pendle Hill, West Pennine moors, Grindleton Fell, and the Bowland moors.

Our time to leave comes when the track receives some wider verges as it winds down above Bookil Gill Beck on the left. Double back through a gate and go a few yards downstream to ford the beck, from where a clear green track heads away. As the beck swings more steeply down to the left, the track contours around a pasture to run on to a gateway below a barn. Head straight on, past a couple of trees on the brow to descend to a gate. The clear track continues most pleasantly down to descend a spur above a flat strath. Through the stile cross to a footbridge by a ford on Long Preston Beck, and slant steeply up the bank to the top of the wood. Look back here up the valley of Long Preston Beck to see the weirdly sculpted limestone tors above Settle.

New Pasture Plantation is owned by the Woodland Trust, and visitors are welcome. *Just yards beyond the access stile take another stile to forsake the now walled New Pasture Lane. Aim directly away from the corner, on the brow locating a stile ahead.* Long Preston is suddenly spread out beneath us, backed by Pendle Hill. *Descend right to another stile, the way being quite obvious now as stiles lead us on. Diagonally across a couple more fields, a crossroads of paths is reached at a wall-corner. Over the stile either descend left to a stile onto a lane, or, go straight ahead across a couple more fields to find a corner-stile onto Green Gate Lane. Turn left to finish on the green.*

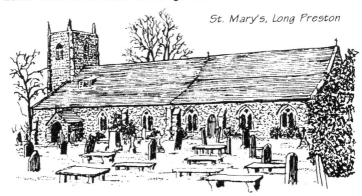

St. Mary's, Long Preston

OTTERBURN MOOR

START Otterburn   Grid ref. SD 883577

DISTANCE 5 ½ miles

ORDNANCE SURVEY MAPS
1:50,000
Landranger 103 - Blackburn & Burnley
1:25,000
Outdoor Leisure 10 - Yorkshire Dales South *or*
Pathfinder 661 - Skipton & Hellifield

ACCESS Otterburn is equidistant from Airton, Hellifield and Bell Busk. There is room for several cars to park between the beck and buildings, just upstream of the bridge, or downstream on the west bank.

An upland ramble with barely any uphill work. Good views from between rolling green foothills.

Otterburn is a sleepy farming hamlet in a fold of the hills, off the beaten track and a million miles from Malham. On the Airton road is Hurries Farm, which offers farm visits at certain times of year - check at an information centre. When the local inhabitants set out for church, they took the route we are using as far as Scosthrop Lane. This old way, known for obvious reasons as Kirk Gait, continues straight on to Kirkby Malham (see WALK 10)

☐ **Leave the junction by the bridge along the unsignposted lane following Otterburn Beck upstream past farm buildings. Almost immediately it becomes a wide track, and beyond a gate it runs free alongside the beck.** *Otterburn Beck is a lively watercourse, and during our acquaintance it performs several modest falls over exposed rocks.*

On approaching another gate, leave the track by a gate on the right, and from it head half-left across the field to pick up a track rising towards a line of trees. From there head across to the top side of the wood in front, then accompany its upper boundary to a gate. Head straight across the field to a stile in the far corner, ignoring a neighbouring stile in the right-hand wall. Follow this wall away in the same direction as before, and when it parts company continue over the brow of the field. This modest brow is a super vantage point, with the Barden Moor skyline over to the right featuring prominently. **Pick out a stile in the wall ahead, bearing left towards it to emerge onto Scosthrop Lane.** Here we take leave of the Kirk Gait, which forges straight on over the stile opposite.

Turn left up the lane only as far as a walled farm-road striking off to the left. Head along its undulating course, which leads unerringly to the remote farm buildings at Orms Gill Green. Features of interest are the large limekiln by the path, and a surprising waterfall where the lively beck escapes from confinement under the farm into trees below.

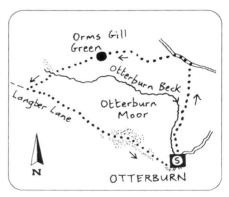

Pass around the back of the farm buildings and stay on the drive up the field behind. At the second cattle-grid after the farm the track becomes completely unenclosed, here leave it by heading half-left across the extensive pasture. Aim for the bottom of the band of trees that appears ahead: as we near them Otterburn Beck appears down to the left, and where these two features meet, a stile is found in the very corner. From it the beck is crossed to an isolated signpost at a crossroads of footpaths: opt for the one climbing the slope behind. At the top it peters out, but continue on a sheep-trod past a wall-corner and then slope down to a stile in the wall ahead. This is one of two walls enclosing the green road of Langber Lane. Langber Lane is a splendid green road running across the hills towards Settle. Our walk makes use of its eastern section. We join it with extensive views to the south-west across the Ribble Valley and down to Pendle Hill and the Bowland moors.

Turn left along this wide byway, enjoying a short-lived green lane cameo. Its demise comes when the right-hand wall parts company. Cross the stile and remain faithful to the left-hand wall: though pathless, the hollowed way by the wall confirms a historic nature. Take in another stile in a fence before arriving at a gate by a wall-junction. From the vicinity of Hellifield Moor Top the panorama includes Rye Loaf Hill, Kirkby Fell, Pikedaw, Malham Moor, Great Whernside, the Cracoe Fell-Crookrise heights, Flasby Fell and Pendle Hill.

On the other side of the gate a track is picked up leading from the small building on the left, and it takes us down through the pasture to a gate. Here it disappears, but resumes its journey from the gate at the bottom of this field. Now entering a plantation the track continues without problem through the trees, emerging as a wide enclosed track known as Dacre Lane to descend very gently into Otterburn. On reaching the road turn left to round a corner to return to the junction by the bridge.

The limekiln,
Orms Gill Green

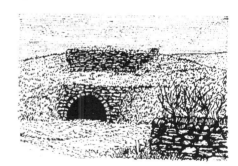

The bridge,
Otterburn

10

KIRKBY MALHAM

START Airton   Grid ref. SD 902591

DISTANCE 4 ¼ miles

ORDNANCE SURVEY MAPS
1:50,000
Landranger 98 - Wensleydale & Upper Wharfedale
          103 - Blackburn & Burnley
1:25,000
Outdoor Leisure 10 - Yorkshire Dales South

ACCESS Start from the village centre. Parking can be found alongside (but not on) the green, or by the road through the village. The Skipton-Malham bus serves Airton.

A gentle ramble over rolling hills, with a superb riverbank walk. For notes on Airton please refer to WALK 11.

☐ **Leave Airton's green by the telephone box at the south-west corner, crossing straight over the main road and up the lane opposite, signposted to Hellifield.** *This attractive corner is Town End - note the old water pump by the roadside just past Manor Farm.* **Shortly after the last buildings take a gate on the right, with another one just behind it.** *Already, we have a first view of Malham Cove ahead.* **Head away along the field-edge, transferring to the other side of a fence when the wall turns away. Here a sunken way continues on to a barn (1862 datestone on window lintel), passing to its left to emerge onto Scosthrop Lane.**

Turn left up this pleasant lane. *A boundary stone is passed, inscribed with the names of the parishes it divides, namely Airton and Scosthrop (now very faint), which is really itself part of Airton.* **A more level section is encountered.** *There is a seat in a fine spot here where a green walled way leads to the quarry on the right -*

Rye Loaf Hill looks impressively high, ahead of us. **A slight descent leads to two stiles directly opposite each other.** *From here to Kirkby Malham our walk follows an old way known as Kirk Gait. As its name suggests, it is the route taken by the good folk of Otterburn (see WALK 9) to reach the parish church. A glimpse at an OS map confirms the practical, direct way they chose.*

Opt for the stile on the right and climb by the wall. *Enjoy a view back to Pendle Hill and the Craven lowlands, and east to the Barden Moor edges and Flasby Fell. Over the wall, note the impressive stone arch at the site of an old quarry.* **Pass left of a small wood to a stile. Continue over the brow of Warber Hill, and down by the wall leading away.** *This descent gives a good view of the general setting of Malhamdale, with all the hills around the valley head to be seen.*

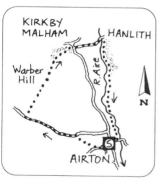

Features include: Rye Loaf Hill, Kirkby Fell, Pikedaw, Fountains Fell, Malham Cove, Malham Moor, the portals of Gordale Scar, Weets Top, Hetton Common Head, Hanlith Moor, and right in front of us, the old Kirk Gait.

Go down to a stile at the bottom, beyond which is a tiny beck. From it leave the wall and bear across the field along a conspicuous groove sloping left. At the fence at the far end Kirkby Malham is revealed quite dramatically at our feet, with the *church tower pre-eminent.* **Go left to a stile, crossing straight over a farm track and descending steeply outside a plantation. From the stile at the bottom, slant down to one in the wall opposite, continuing the direction to a small gate to enter the trees below. Steps descend to a footbridge on Kirkby Beck, then up onto a lane by the church.** *For notes on Kirkby Malham, refer to WALK 13.*

Turn right, over the crossroads by the inn and down the lane (Green Gate) opposite. *On the left is a cottage with a 1637 datestone and mullioned windows.* **The lane runs down to Hanlith Bridge.** *Prominent just opposite is Hanlith Hall, which dates back in parts to 1668.* **Cross the bridge to a stile and accompany the river downstream. The Aire is close company for a considerable stretch of this parkland country. On reaching two neighbouring stiles the path short-cuts a bend of the river. Follow the wall away, keeping* *straight on when it leaves us, to pass a fence corner leading to two footbridges ahead. Whilst the left-hand one also leads to Airton Bridge, opt for the larger one over the Aire itself. Cross it and make for a stile in the wall downstream. Continue on to the start of the old mill-race at another footbridge at the old weir.*

The path is now sandwiched between mill-race and river, remaining so to wind round to Airton Mill. The walk alongside the leat is an interesting mini-history trail. Largely dry but still marshy, and with evidences of old workings. The imposing mill, which once spun cotton, is well preserved after conversion into individual flats. *Pass round to the right, into the car park and out onto a road. The bridge is just down to the left, and the green just up to the right.* Returning to the green, a cottage on the right bears a 1696 datestone, and many dovecotes in its central gable, while on the left is the Friends Meeting House dated 1700.

Hanlith Bridge

BELL BUSK

START Airton   Grid ref. SD 902591

DISTANCE 5 miles

ORDNANCE SURVEY MAPS
1:50,000
Landranger 103 - Blackburn & Burnley
1:25,000
Outdoor Leisure 10 - Yorkshire Dales South *or*
Pathfinder 661 - Skipton & Hellifield

ACCESS Start from the village centre. Parking can be found alongside (but not on) the green, or by the road through the village. The Skipton-Malham bus serves Airton.

Airton is a tidy village, larger and more spacious than Malham. There are many old houses tucked away, and several 17th century datestones can be found. The main feature is the triangular green on which stands the 'squatter's house'. In times past this would be the home of some local unfortunate, previously of no-fixed-abode, who had fallen lucky with the powers-that-be. Alongside are the stone posts of the former village stocks. On the northern edge of the village is 17th century Scosthrop Manor.

☐ **Leave Airton's green by the telephone box at the south-west corner, crossing straight over the main road and up the lane opposite, signposted to Hellifield.** *This attractive corner is Town End - note the old water pump by the roadside just past Manor Farm.* **Turn off at the first opportunity along a road to the left (signposted Hellifield). This is also soon forsaken, this time along Kirk Syke Lane to the right.** *This farm track is followed throughout its entire length, enjoyings views over its hedgerows to the Barden edges and Flasby Fell.* **It runs straight on past the farm at Kirk Syke, and on to a grouping of its barns.**

A change of character here sees it advance straight on into a field. Keep straight on a part sunken way, passing an old quarry, two ponds and a barn to emerge into a field. Head straight on to a gate ahead, with the fence switching to the left to reach the next gate. Follow the fence down to the prominent barn, behind which is a bridge over Otterburn Beck. From it a clear track leads through a bomb-site, past some barns onto the lane in Bell Busk.

On the right here is Raven Flatts, a fine 17th century house with mullioned windows. The scattered community of Bell Busk stands at the confluence of Otterburn Beck with the Aire, and is dominated by the railway. A century ago there were mills spinning silk here. Bell Busk's seven-arch viaduct is a low structure spanning the Aire on the Leeds-Morecambe line.

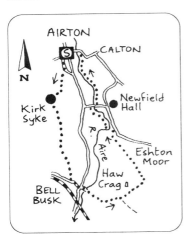

Turn left along this lane. On the grassy sward here is a free standing slender boundary stone, inscribed 'K' (Kirkby Malham) and 'G' (Gargrave). *At the junction cross the road bridge over the beck and fork right immediately along a lesser lane to cross a bridge over the Aire.* Directly above, prominent Haw Crag awaits. *The lane heads uphill, now with a rougher surface.* Over to the right the viaduct is revealed. *On levelling out we pass an isolated house, and after a farm drive the way becomes rougher, turning sharp left to climb again.*

Leave the lane at the next sharp bend right, taking the gate directly ahead to enter the pasture containing Haw Crag. A faint green trackway heads straight up the slope to fade on the edge of the old quarry. The path continues along the fence-side to the gate at the end. Few will resist the rim of the quarry leading to the Ordnance column marking the highest point. Haw Crag's dramatic appearance was enhanced by quarrying a century ago, and the trig. point (S5308) stands at 676ft atop the steep drop. In addition to the panorama depicted opposite, the Bowland moors, Pendle Hill, and the South Pennines are well represented.

The corner gate, meanwhile, has a dubious stile alongside. Head directly across the field behind to find a guidepost on the site of a former fence corner: here the Pennine Way is joined and followed all the way back to Airton. This area known as Eshton Moor has long since lost any claim to such description. *Take the left branch (no path) down to two stiles in the bottom of the field, then follow the wall away as far as a bend. Now head straight down the centre of this vast field.* Directly ahead, the winding Aire is our target. The large house in view is Newfield Hall, a Holiday Fellowship centre. Also in view are Calton, behind it, and Airton itself. *As the walls converge alongside a road, this narrow way leads down to a stile on the left, and a small beck leads to a footbridge over the river.*

From the bridge follow the riverbank upstream, briefly entering the encroaching wood before forging on to reach Newfield Bridge. A stile to its left empties onto the road. Cross the bridge and take a stile on the left to rejoin the river once more. From a stile by a gate follow the wall straight ahead, nearing the river again at two stiles in quick succession. At this point the river is particularly narrow, sufficient for a reasonable athlete to safely leap - don't! *From the second stile leave the river again for a stile in the next wall along, and then head across the large pasture, closing in on the river as Airton Bridge comes into view. A stile admits to the road.*

Alongside the bridge is the substantial mill, converted to residential use. Note the bell still in place. It stands on the site of a mill owned by the Canons of Bolton Priory, in Wharfedale. *Cross the bridge to climb the lane back onto the green.* A cottage on the right bears a 1696 datestone and many dovecotes in its central gable, while on the left is the Friends Meeting House of 1700.

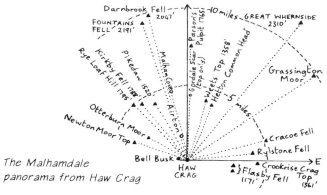

The Malhamdale panorama from Haw Crag

12

CALTON MOOR

START Calton   Grid ref. SD 908591

DISTANCE 8½ miles

ORDNANCE SURVEY MAPS
1:50,000
Landranger 98 - Wensleydale & Upper Wharfedale
            103 - Blackburn & Burnley
1:25,000
Outdoor Leisure 10 - Yorkshire Dales South

ACCESS Start from the cul-de-sac street, just off the Airton-Hetton road. There is ample roadside parking taking care not to block any private access. Calton is only ten minutes walk from Airton, which is served by Skipton-Malham bus.

This is an ideal Bank holiday walk for Malhamdale, for while you won't entirely avoid the crowds, you'll miss most of them.

Calton is a sleepy hamlet, but with some history: the original Calton Hall was the home of John Lambert, one of Cromwell's major generals during the Civil War.

☐ **At the end of the short-lived street, turn right along a rough lane past Nelsons Farm.** *This runs on between hedgerows with nice views over the lower dale to Pendle Hill.* **At a modern barn bear left, the way rising to quickly emerge into a field. Keep straight on by the wall, and when this and the track fade, advance with a line of trees to find a stile in the corner. Beyond this keep on a hollowed green way with a fence on the left.** *Views ahead open out to bring in Pendle Hill, while nearer is a peep of Flasby Fell with Barden Moor and the Cracoe Fell monument over to the left.* **Another such stile is met at the end: bear left across the field to the barn of Farlands Laithe.** *The Barden Moor/Flasby Fell skyline is now a wondrous prospect.* **From a ladder-stile to its left, continue past barn and** fence corner, and aim directly for the farm of Cowper Cote ahead. After dropping to an intervening trickle head up the field to a gate in a short section of wall above the farm.

Advance towards the other buildings, but then turn up the large field and head away on a faint tractor way towards the top, bearing right near the end to find a gateway just short of the corner. The faint way continues, bearing right to stay near the fence and an embankment. Beyond another gate again remain near the fence, descending at the end to a gate just above the bottom corner, above a wood. Turn up to the prominent barn of Windros Laithe, going round it to find a stile below the small plantation. This next stage to Smither Gill Laithe is a recent diversion. Before reaching the second plantation, cross the wall on the right and follow it away to the corner. On crossing the wall in front, cut across the bottom corner of the field and into the next field. Now turn along its left side towards the isolated house at Smither Gill Laithe. Pass to its left to follow its drive climbing away to a junction.

Go left towards Way Gill Farm, but without entering its yard, turn into the field on the right and cross to a gate to the right of the house. Bear gently left down the field. Winterburn Reservoir is now laid out ahead. At the bottom a stile admits onto another farm road. This goes left to Higher Cow House, but we leave it before the farm, at a stile on the right. This is another path diversion, avoiding the farmyard and giving better views over the reservoir.

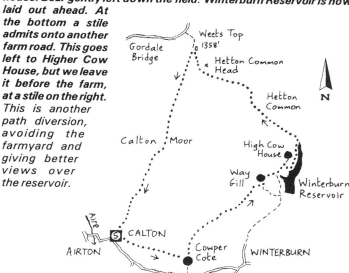

49

Head down the field-side to approach the reservoir. Turn left along the bottom of the field, and on through a couple more above the upper reach of the reservoir, to arrive at a big stone arched bridge over Bordley Beck before it enters the reservoir. Just before it, a stone inscribed 'LLC' indicates that the reservoir was constructed to supply the Leeds-Liverpool Canal at Gargrave.

Winterburn Reservoir is a substantial finger-like sheet of water, and one could at times be forgiven for believing it to be natural. Even the dam with its grass cover seems to blend in well. Now there is an air of neglect, though the keeper's house has recently been restored. A variety of bird-life takes advantage of this peaceful setting. The head of the reservoir points to extensive moor-like terrain. This is a fine spot for a five minute break.

Resume without crossing the bridge by taking a gate on the left (signed Malham), from where a path rises away with the wall through rough pasture. Here begins the lengthy but exceedingly well graded climb to Hetton Common Head and Weets Top. Never far from the wall, the splendid pathway rises to a gate at the top, then curves right through a reedy pasture to another. Through this it fades, but curve up around the field top and along with the wall to a gate in the far corner. Entering the moor proper, the way climbs by a long gone wall to a gateway. Rise away, initially faintly before picking up a clearer path. Over to the right is the barn of Ray Gill Laithe, forever etched in the author's uncomplicated mind as the grid reference example on the old 1" sheet 'Wensleydale', his first ever map. At a mere 40p, the 10% rise to 44p on those trusty, red-covered classics is also recalled as a fair old price hike!

Rising increasingly pleasurably up (with limestone hills viewed over to the right, and Great Whernside easing its broad shoulders into place), *the path meets a wall coming up from the left, and together rise to a brow on Hetton Common Head.* Ahead now is the long awaited view into Malhamdale, and it's a cracker: the show-stealer, though,

Weets Cross

is the unexpected appearance of mighty Ingleborough in the gap between Grizedales and Fountains Fell. The modest summit of Hetton Common Head is just up to the right, marked by a small cairn. **Five minutes ahead is the 'parent' top Weets Top, marked by an OS column, and the path duly runs thereto.** Weets Top is one of the finest viewpoints in the area, with most of the features in the southern Dales in sight. Quite a number of township boundaries meet here and the restored cross, just over the wall yards to the left, serves to mark this point.

Leave the gate there by doubling back sharply to the left, on a clear path heading down the moor with the wall close by on the right. Within minutes a guidepost indicates a crossroads of ways: the clearest path goes over the stile on the right bound for Kirkby Malham. Our way, however, keeps straight on, a thinner but still clear path commencing the prolonged descent of Calton Moor. This proves to be a splendid leg-stretcher, forever losing height at the most gentle of rates. Views to the left feature Barden Moor, and to the right the Malhamdale hills around Kirkby Fell.

Never straying far from the right-hand wall, the path eventually reaches a stile in a cross-wall. Beyond that the limestone wall on the right soon parts company, but the grassy trackway keeps straight on over a large sheep pasture, curving round to the right to descend above a wooded gill on the left. Airton's houses appear just ahead, as shortly do one or two of Calton's. **Descending to a corner by some sheep pens the track becomes enclosed and continues as a leafy rough lane. Fording the sometimes dry beck it quickly climbs back to the road end where the walk began.**

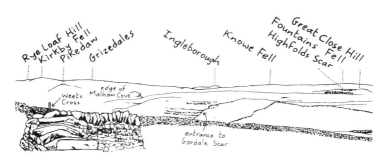

Looking west from Weets Top

AIRE HEAD

START Malham   Grid ref. SD 900626

DISTANCE 3 ¾ miles

ORDNANCE SURVEY MAPS
1:50,000
Landranger 98 - Wensleydale & Upper Wharfedale
1:25,000
Outdoor Leisure 10 - Yorkshire Dales South

ACCESS Start from the village centre. There is a large car park by the National Park Centre. Served by bus from Skipton.

☐ *Leave the information centre for the village, but within yards take a stile on the right, where the road and beck meet. With a wall separating us, follow the beck downstream, crossing a stile, then Tranlands Beck, and another stile. As the beck swings away to the left, continue straight ahead to arrive at the emerging waters (or not!) of Aire Head Springs.*

Aire Head Springs is the point of resurgence of the stream that last saw the light of day at Water Sinks, high on the moor (see WALK 3). It is not, therefore, the source of the Aire, but it is certainly the first naming of the river Aire. Almost immediately downstream, its waters - which after heavy rain become one mighty spring - join the newly merged Malham and Gordale Becks to flow in unison as the Aire.

From the stile just beyond continue alongside the wall. The next stile returns us nearer the river, by now having merged with the beck. An improving path leads above the old millpond. Now a bird haven, the extensive pond remains in good condition, as does the still full leat which we follow along to the mill. It leads unfailingly on to Scalegill Mill, the former manorial mill, now a private dwelling.

There has been a mill on this site at least since the 11th century, as it was mentioned in the Domesday Book. It has been used in turn for processing corn, wool, flax and cotton, which in the early 19th century made it Kirkby Malham's major employer. The waterwheel was removed in 1925, when turbines - still in use - were installed for generating electricity. **Pass round the top side of it to a kissing-gate above its entrance gate.**

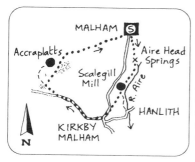

Instead of following the drive away, take the pronounced grass rake sloping up to a stile. This is the old millworkers' route from the village. Note the attractive grouping of Hanlith over to the left. **Head half-right to another stile and straight on towards the road as it enters Kirkby Malham. Don't join it, but walk parallel with it over the wall. A stile by a gate at the end admits to the road, but to avoid traffic on a narrow bend, go left along the walled lane. This bends round to the Hanlith road, turning right on it to enter the village centre.**

Kirkby Malham is, ecclesiastically at least, the main village of Malhamdale, although most visitors to the valley drive through almost without notice on their way to the tourist mecca of Malham. This tiny village is however worth a brief exploration, and not surprisingly the parish church is of most interest. Dedicated to St. Michael the Archangel, this highly attractive building dates from the 15th century and was restored a century ago, thanks mainly to Walter Morrison of Malham Tarn House: his memorial can be seen in the church. Also of note are a Norman font and a 16th century German window. Oliver Cromwell is reputed to have signed the register as witnessing a marriage during his stay in the district during the Civil War.

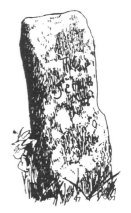

Milestone on Scosthrop Lane

53

Scalegill Mill

In the churchyard is the base of an ancient preaching cross, and near the lych-gate are the former village stocks. The church is sandwiched between two other buildings of note, namely the inn at the bridge-end and the immensely attractive vicarage. The Victoria *is a pleasant hostelry which does its best to waylay Malham-bound visitors, and features a sundial dated MDCCCXL above the door. The old vicarage has a three-storeyed porch dated 1622, and was restored in 1866. Running alongside is Kirkby Beck, which joins the Aire a good quarter mile from the village. Further up the lane is the Old Hall.*

From the crossroads by the pub head up the back lane past the church, and round to a T-junction. Turn up the lane to the left, the severe gradients ensuring height is gained rapidly. *Compensation is found in the extensive views, including the Malham scene over to the right: ahead is Pikedaw. This provides an excellent insight into the topography of the area, with Kirkby Fell and Weets Top guarding each side of the valley, and Malham, the Cove and the heights of the moor in between.*

A farm road to New Close is passed before reaching the track forking right to Acraplatts. *Easily missed on the left here is an old milestone, inscribed 'to Settle 5ms.' and obverse 'to Kirkby 1m'.*

Follow the farm road along, with bracing views over the entire upper dale now: the prospect of rugged Pikedaw is particularly impressive. *Just past a gate take a stile on the right. Descend the field to another stile, then pass a ruined barn to a slate slab footbridge over Tranlands Beck (again).*

From it head across the field without losing height, deflected left by a wall to a stile and another tiny beck. From it slope up gently across the field to another stile. This is a superb moment, as Malham's setting is revealed in its amphitheatre of hills. *Follow the wall heading down to a barn. Two more stiles see us in a large pasture.*

While enjoying the great, sweeping vista, note the strip lynchets on the opposite slope between Cove and village, and the remarkably haphazard pattern of the drystone walls behind. *Drop down to find a gate in the very bottom. From the stile by it an enclosed pathway heads away, quickly becoming a broader track which leads all the way down into Malham village, emerging next to the car park.*

Kirkby Malham

55

14

GORDALE SCAR & MASTILES LANE

START Malham   Grid ref. SD 900626

DISTANCE 9½ miles

ORDNANCE SURVEY MAPS
1:50,000
Landranger 98 - Wensleydale & Upper Wharfedale
1:25,000
Outdoor Leisure 10 - Yorkshire Dales South

ACCESS Start from the village centre. There is a large car park by the National Park Centre. Served by bus from Skipton.

This walk is particularly suitable for breaking down into two separate shorter rambles; by using the traffic free Smearbottoms Lane (becoming Hawthorns Lane) as a link back to and out of Malham, for the two walks respectively.

It should be noted that at Gordale Scar one needs to partake of a short climb on rock - this is a fairly simple task with ample handholds, but may nevertheless be outside the scope of less-agile walkers. It is beyond all non-amphibious walkers after a good deal of rain. The alternatives are mentioned during the text.

☐ **From the car park head into the village, crossing the beck either by a footbridge by the forge, or by the road bridge and doubling back to follow the beck downstream. The short lane ends at a gate, from where a broad path heads across the fields. At a double kissing-gate the path swings left to a barn, (the fainter way straight ahead is our return route) crosses to the left of the wall and continues in the same direction.** *The outer portals of Gordale await, but as yet reveal nothing of the grandeur to come: Malham Cove, however, shows itself off back over the village.*

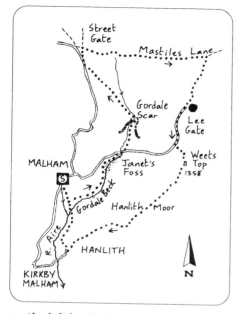

Soon, on entering a delightful section of woodland, the charming waterfall of Janet's Foss is reached. Legend has it that Janet, local fairy queen, had a cave behind the falls. What is more certain is that this wood provides a rich habitat for a wide variety of flora and fauna: an information board is provided. *Here the path breaks off left to emerge onto the road to Gordale. Turn right along it for a short distance, crossing the beck (by way of the old bridge if you wish) and arriving at a gate on the left just before Gordale House.* The Augustinian canons of Bolton Priory once owned Gordale, and traces of foundations close to the path mark the site of a building where they held a manorial court. *A well trodden path heads across the pasture to the unmistakable cliffs of Gordale Scar, which converge as we enter the dark confines.*

Gordale Scar is probably the most awe-inspiring single feature of the Yorkshire Dales. Unlike the Cove at Malham, which bares all on first sighting, the Scar has a far more intriguing nature, waiting for the visitor to turn the final corner before impressing him to the full. Once in its depths the grandeur of the overhanging cliffs up above can initially be a little too daunting to fully appreciate the waterfalls: the upper fall spills in spectacular fashion through a circular hole in the rocks. The water is that of Gordale Beck, being funnelled from the lonely moors to the green valley. Like the cove, this is a valley cut back from the Mid Craven Fault, formed by erosive action of ice and glacial meltwater, rather than being a collapsed cave. Turn a corner and it's there, is there no escape?

The way out is by negotiating the rock to the left of the lower falls. It is a straightforward short scramble with plentiful hand-holds, but nevertheless care is necessary - please don't fall on anyone. If it proves impassable, hang your head low and use an alternative: either latch onto WALK 1 (short return via Cove) or regain the current walk by turning up the lane past Gordale House to the Weets lane. On gaining the top of the climb, pause to survey the tremendous scene in this magnificent amphitheatre, including a better prospect of the upper fall dropping through its window.

Having clambered up, the stony path clings to the left side of the gorge, passing the upper falls and breaking out onto green pastures once more. Running straight ahead is the upper Gordale Valley. Beyond a stile the path becomes sketchy, but this matters little for the way appears fairly obvious as it passes through low outcrops. A long line of low outcrops deflect our path to the left, and a long trek ensues before arriving at a stile onto the moor road to Malham Tarn. Follow this right, keeping on a broad track by the wall when it swings away, to arrive at the historic crossroads of Street Gate. An old sign points the way - our way also - towards Grassington.

Gordale Scar

Arrival at Street Gate signals the commencement of our march along Mastiles Lane. *Mastiles Lane is probably the best known of the district's old roads. The classic green lane was used by the monks of Fountains Abbey to cross from Kilnsey to their valuble sheep-rearing pastures in the Malham area, indeed, continuing ultimately to their lands in Borrowdale, in distant Cumberland. Packmen and drovers would also* have taken advantage of it. *The lane is at its most inspiring when fully enclosed by walls, though the monks would not have known it that way. Several large boulders incorporated into the lane's north wall are boundary stones separating Malham and Bordley.*

The walking is easy and pleasant as the track clings to the right-hand wall. Some sections are well rutted, though being largely open it matters not to our steps. A big dip takes in the upper reaches of Gordale Beck. *Up to the left is Middle House, while an ancient cross base is passed on a brow just above the track.* **At a gate the way becomes confined, and shortly before the next gate in the lane we leave it by a gate on the right, where a good track doubles back alongside a fence.**

This track becomes fully enclosed to drop down past the isolated Lee Gate Farm, with whose access road we merge to join the head of Smearbottoms Lane: head along this undulating strip of tarmac. *Ahead, distantly, is the Ribble Valley between Pendle Hill and Grindleton Fell.* **Leave the lane by the second walled track on the left, which makes a short climb (it's all downhill after this brief**

Janet's
Foss

interruption) to Weets Cross. Through the gate adjacent to it will be found, just up to the left, the Ordnance column marking Weets Top. Weets Top is one of the finest viewpoints in the area, with most features in the southern Dales in sight: WALK 12 has more detail on this. Quite a number of old township boundaries meet here and the restored cross serves to mark this point.

Returning to the gate, a good path heads away from it beginning a gentle descent of the moor. Soon a guidepost at a crossroads of paths indicates a stile in the wall on the right, and from it a path heads across Hanlith Moor, a grand stride out with a succession of marker-posts serving to confirm the route. Far ahead are Pendle Hill, the Ribble Valley, Grindleton Fell, and the Bowland moors. *Eventually a gate is reached, through which the rough track of Windy Pike Lane leads unfailingly down into Hanlith.* During the descent Malham village and Cove are regular features, as well as a wide sweep of most of Malhamdale proper: note across on Kirkby Fell and Pikedaw a dramatic change from gritstone to limestone. There is also a fine prospect of Kirkby Malham across the river, the church tower being a prominent feature.

Do not drop down all the way to the river, but at the second sharp bend in Hanlith go straight on to a stile on the right, above a farm. Cross a small enclosure, out above the farm to contour across the field. Malham Cove is directly ahead now. Across the river note the distinctive Anglian strip lynchets (cultivation terraces) beneath the dale's school. *At the end of the field we are channeled into a stile, to continue along the top of a wood. In the next field a vague path contours the indentation of a tiny beck before descending another field to a footbridge over Gordale Beck, by the confluence with Malham Beck. From the fence behind it aim well to the left of the barn ahead, and at the economy-size stile our outward leg is rejoined. Retrace those first few steps back into the village.*

Clapper Bridge on Gordale Beck, Mastiles Lane

15
WINTERBURN RESERVOIR

START Winterburn   Grid ref. SD 935586

DISTANCE 6¼ miles

ORDNANCE SURVEY MAPS
1:50,000
Landranger 98 - Wensleydale & Upper Wharfedale
            103 - Blackburn & Burnley
1:25,000
Outdoor Leisure 10 - Yorkshire Dales South

ACCESS Winterburn is astride the Hetton-Airton road: there is ample parking just off the through road skirting the hamlet.

An easy circuit of a lovely sheet of water, returning via a splendid old house. Winterburn is a small farming community set in an attractive fold of the hills. Here is a former chapel of 1703, one of the first Independent chapels. It was restored early this century, and as Chapel House is now a private residence.

☐ **From the T-junction head up the dead-end road through the heart of the hamlet, passing the venerable Rookery Farm on the right. On reaching a cattle-grid it becomes a private farm road, crossing a length of pasture by the beck to arrive at a bridge. Cross it and follow the road along to the right, still alongside the beck. After a while it gradually climbs above the beck to arrive at the reservoir keeper's house. The grassy dam of Winterburn Reservoir appears ahead now. Our route however does not quite reach the house, for we turn sharp left up the farm road which leads circuitously but unerringly to Way Gill Farm.**

Without entering its yard, turn into the field on the right and cross to a gate to the right of the house. Bear gently left down the field. Winterburn Reservoir is now outspread ahead. At the bottom is a

61

*stile onto another farm road. This goes left to **Higher Cow House,** but we leave it before the farm, at a stile on the right. This path diversion avoids the farmyard and gives much better views over the reservoir. **Head down the field-side to approach the reservoir. Turn left along the bottom of the field, and on through a couple more above the upper reach of the reservoir to arrive at a big stone arched bridge over Bordley Beck before it enters the reservoir.** Just before it, a stone inscribed 'LLC' indicates that the reservoir was con-structed to supply the Leeds-Liverpool Canal at Gargrave.*

Winterburn Reservoir is a substantial finger-like sheet of water, and at times could easily be mistaken for being natural. Even the dam with its grass cover seems to blend in well. Now there is an air of neglect, though the keeper's house has recently been restored. A variety of bird-life take advantage of this peaceful setting. The Winterburn valley is split into two very different sections by the reservoir: downstream is a deep, heavily-wooded confine, while the head of the reservoir points to more extensive, moor-like terrain.

Across the bridge is a large expanse of rough pasture, and an indistinct path heads up it, half-left for a few yards only and then turning right to rise gradually. *Ever broadening views over the reservoir are backed by a distant but prominent Pendle Hill.* **The path slowly levels out to arrive at a gate in a descending wall at the head of Moor Lane.** *This is something of a Piccadilly Circus of footpaths, for a guidepost points in no less than five directions, namely to Bordley, Hetton, Threshfield, Winterburn and Malham. Don't go astray here!*

Pass through the gate then leave immediately by a gate on the right. Cross another rough pasture to a conspicuous gap in the line of trees ahead. Re-emerging, a thin path heads across an immense tract of rough pasture towards a small cluster of trees surrounding Long House Farm. *Now we have a good prospect of the wooded* *lower valley, along with Cracoe and Flasby Fells, the South Pennines, Pendle Hill, Grindleton Fell and the Bowland moors.* **Converging with the wall across to the right, a barn conversion is passed: stay outside the farm's confines, and after a gate continue past Long House to another gate.**

A large dome-like pasture is entered, with no path nor sign of exit. Aim diagonally away from the gate, and straight over the brow of the field using the graceful peak of Sharp Haw as an infallible guide. Passing a wall corner on the right, descend to the far corner and use a gateway a few yards to the right. From it follow the wall on the left, passing two barns at Owslin Laithe and remaining with the same wall to emerge onto the Hetton-Winterburn road.

Cross to the gate immediately opposite and head down to a gate in the corner, then continuing by the wall to eventually reach another gate at the far end. *Enjoy a closing look back at the rugged skyline from Cracoe Fell to Flasby Fell as the Malhamdale hills of Kirkby Fell and Pikedaw appear ahead.* **Head away again with the wall now on the right, and from a gate in a fence bear right to drop to a gate in the corner. Now simply accompany the wall on the right down onto the lane opposite Friars Head.** *This superb 17th century house is the most interesting in the district, and looks entirely lost in this remote setting. Its south front is a remarkably intricate four-bayed facade of mullioned windows. The monks of Furness Abbey had a grange here, and farm life still thrives (Illustrated on page 71).* **Turn right along the lane for a short walk back into Winterburn.**

Rookery Farm, Winterburn

63

16

BORDLEY

START Boss Moor   Grid ref. SD 955619

DISTANCE 7 ½ miles

ORDNANCE SURVEY MAPS
1:50,000
Landranger 98 - Wensleydale & Upper Wharfedale
1:25,000
Outdoor Leisure 10 - Yorkshire Dales South

ACCESS To reach Boss Moor, first go to Hetton. From the bus
shelter at the Rylstone junction take the Cracoe road, and after
100 yards a lane forks left, signposted 'Bordley 4'. Half-way
up, it emerges onto open moor. Almost at once an obvious
parking place is seen on the right, with a guidepost and an old
quarry in close proximity.

◻ *Before even starting, take a glance over the wall for a most
complete view of Winterburn Reservoir, with Pendle Hill directly
behind.* **The walk commences with a gentle stroll along the lane
towards Bordley, as far as the phone box and farm at Lainger.**
Lainger House bears a 1673 datestone. **Here leave the lane by the
farm track down to the left, accompanying a beck to cross the main
beck in the valley bottom. Take a stile on the right to follow Bordley
Beck upstream, over another stile and then across to a gate to the
left of a small group of trees.**

*The deeply-confined valley of Bordley Beck is a charming location,
hidden from the outside world. It forms the upper reach of the
Winterburn valley (see WALK 15) and boasts colourful bracken
slopes.* **From the gate head across the part reedy pasture high
above the beck. Ahead is the isolated farm of Bordley Hall. Don't
return to the beck, but bear left to drop to a side-stream. Follow it
left a short way to a ladder-stile (the path has been diverted here).
Head away with the wall, picking up an incoming track to reach a
wall-corner level with the farm. There is a bubbling spring here.**

Turn right with the track to a gate to arrive behind all the buildings.
Just ahead is a guidepost, which sends us left, climbing the steep
field to a gate. In the large field behind, a gate appears in the top
wall. With the gradient easing, head half-right to locate a hidden
stile in the corner. All around, limestone country now dominates.
The dogs of Bordley are likely to be heard before the buildings are
seen. *From the stile a farm track is joined heading for Bordley.*
Bordley is entered between a house (1664 datestone incorporated)
and a barn directly across the last smaller field.

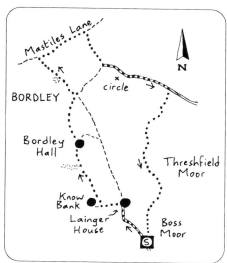

Bordley is a farming
hamlet standing at a
breezy 1100 feet above
sea level. Its remote-
ness is stressed by the
fact that several lanes
head towards it, but
none actually reach it
as fully made up roads.
The solid stone build-
ings are spread around
a large green, which is
workman-like rather
than picturesque. The
hamlet shelters from
the weather's worst
excesses by virtue of
its position in a hollow.
A plethora of footpaths
and bridleways radiate
from the centre.

Turn briefly left in the hamlet, but ignore the walled track, and turn
right on a track to the top corner. A clear track heads away from
the gate in front of a barn. In a few yards take a lesser track right,
rising gently above a wall-corner and on beneath a small plantation.
We are now well and truly in the midst of archetypal, rolling
limestone uplands. Note the pronounced 'horseshoe' earthwork
mound curving round below, crossed and ignored by a modern
wall. The OS map depicts it as any other field boundary, though it
is clearly of older origin, possibly medieval.

The track remains faint but clear as it swings to the right beyond
the plantation to join Mastiles Lane through a crumbling wall.
Mastiles Lane is probably the most famous of the district's old

Limekiln at Height Laithe

roads. *The classic green lane was used by the monks of Fountains Abbey to cross from Kilnsey to their valuble sheep-rearing pastures in the Malham area. The lane is at its most inspiring when fully enclosed by walls, even though the monks would never have known it that way.*

Head right along the lane: beyond a gate (optimistically signed 'Kilnsey 2 miles') it hugs the left wall to become enclosed again at Mastiles Gate. Here leave the lane by turning right on a faint wall-side track through a hollow, to a crossroads of ways marked by a guidepost. Turn left through a gateway and up the tarmac arm. As this lane levels out, branch across to the right to peer over the wall at a stone circle. *Bordley stone circle is, to say the least, of modest proportions, but anything of such antiquity is worth a minute's detour. Three tightly-huddled stones are all that remains of a larger circle thought to date from the Bronze age.*

Bordley Stone Circle (Pendle Hill beyond)

Rejoin the lane as it becomes enclosed. *This lane rejoices in no less than four different names during its three mile journey, the length we follow being known as Malham Moor Lane. Ahead is a fine prospect of Simon's Seat across Wharfedale.* ***This quiet way is now trodden for a long half-mile, to the point where guideposts indicate a junction with a bridle-path.*** *By this stage, the great mass of Barden Moor has ousted the more distant Simon's Seat. On leaving the lane, note the conspicuous twin cave entrances of Calf Hole (or Height Cave) a little further down, it has yielded evidences of Bronze age and Iron age man.*

From the gate on the right a string of posts guide us along a level track. At another gate we descend more clearly past the barn of Height Laithe. *Just across the field behind is a splendidly preserved limekiln.* ***Head along an enclosed way to a gate at the far end. From it a track heads right, crossing the marshy beginnings of a small beck to rise to a gate in a fence.*** *Here, pause to look back over the last stage, and to see the broad shoulders of Great Whernside far up Wharfedale.* ***From the gate the track heads across the open moor, again with marker posts assisting. Further marshy sections are likely.***

Threshfield Moor provides extensive views, notably of Great Whernside and the Cracoe and Flasby Fells. ***On reaching a wall, we are channeled through a pleasant walled green way to the next section of moor. Remain with the right-hand wall as far as a gate onto Boss Moor. A good track heads diagonally away from the gate, and with the Bordley lane soon in view, our track avoids it until reaching the old quarries and, all being well, the car.***

Mastiles
Lane

ESHTON

START Gargrave   Grid ref. SD 931541

DISTANCE 5¾ miles

ORDNANCE SURVEY MAPS
1:50,000
Landranger 103 - Blackburn & Burnley
1:25,000
Outdoor Leisure 10 - Yorkshire Dales South *or*
Pathfinder 661 - Skipton & Hellifield

ACCESS Start from the bridge in the village centre. There are two car parks just around the back from the cafe opposite. Gargrave is served by the Skipton-Settle bus, and also by train.

❑ *Gargrave is an attractive village which makes an ideal centre for Malhamdale. Although Skipton, main centre for the southern Dales, is only 10 minutes distant by road, Gargrave has a more intimate Dales atmosphere. The village is split by the busy A65 running through it, though a planned by-pass will change all that, and will also interfere with the route, as it takes the northern side of the village. Lined by shops, the main street widens into a spacious area by the war memorial, and here a sturdy bridge crosses the river to the parish church. Dedicated to St. Andrew, it was restored in 1852: the tower dates from the early 16th century.*

The Pennine Way passes through the heart of the village, and the two central inns provide appropriately placed lunchtime breaks for those midway between youth hostels at Earby and Malham. The Leeds-Liverpool Canal also comes this way, reaching the northern-most point of its 127¼ miles as it meets the National Park boundary. The waterway takes advantage of the Aire Gap to squeeze its way through the Pennines. Our mighty backbone also gives its name to the homespun bus company based in the village, and their orange livery may well be seen threading the local lanes.

From Gargrave to Haw Crag, our route follows that of the Pennine Way, 70 miles into its total of 270 and at the very outset of its 53 miles in the Yorkshire Dales National Park. **Leave the main street along West Street, almost opposite the bridge over the Aire, and at the second car-park continue straight ahead over the canal bridge. Ignore any turn-offs and remain on this leafy by-way (Mark House Lane) for a gradual uphill march: after the demise of the trees on the right, take a stile into the field on the same side.** The lane, a former packhorse way, continues to Bell Busk.

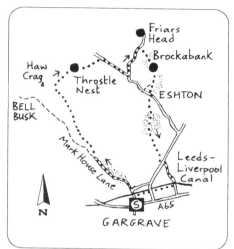

At once the mighty Pennine Way becomes non-existent! **Remain parallel with the lane for a short distance, then strike across the field, past the stump of a solitary tree to a stile in the fence ahead. Advance to the near corner then slant steeply up to a stile above. Continue the climb to the top corner of the plantation on Harrows Hill.** Back over to the right are Cracoe Fell, Flasby Fell and Skipton Moor, with Pendle Hill behind us.

A gate in the fence ahead is ignored in favour of a stile along to the left, from where strike diagonally across the field to another stile. Maintain this course to the wall ahead, and follow it left to a gate in the corner. From it head off diagonally over the brow of the field. The fence corner on OS maps has been replaced by a four-way guidepost. For a while now, the Ordnance column on Haw Crag has been in sight, and as a right of way runs through its field, a 10-minute detour may be deemed worth the effort (see WALK 11).

Our present route still enjoys the main features of the view, finest aspect being that of the Malhamdale scene to the north. **At the guidepost leave the Pennine Way by turning sharp right. Cross straight over a permanent track and advance to the edge of the** *field: down to the left is Throstle Nest Farm, through which the path ran until a recent diversion. Our way now takes a ladder-stile in the wall ahead, at the near edge of a small plantation (not shown as such on the map). Slant down to a stile and gate in the right corner, straight over a farm track, and away along the wall-side to join the farm drive. Go straight ahead on this, over the cattle-grid to run pleasantly out onto a road.* This drive is a fine vantage point for enjoying the prospect of the Barden Moor massif and the shapely tops of Flasby Fell, straight ahead.

Turn right to descend to the junction at Eshton. This is the Malham road, which can be extremely busy on summer weekends - take care. At the junction admire the lovely house of St. Helens: it has five bays and dates from the 18th century. Eshton is a scattered community with no definable centre. It has several other fine buildings, including Eshton House also by this junction, and the Hall, dating from 1827 and now a residential home on the road towards Gargrave. *Escape along the quiet back road towards Winterburn.*

The lane runs on past St. Helen's Well, in a wooded corner on the left as the road runs down to the bridge on Eshton Beck. It was clearly given greater respect in times past, when local people would have placed faith in its healing properties. Nevertheless today it remains a pleasing sight when the water gurgles up into the part man-made pool. Ahead now the engaging prospect of Friars Head is revealed further along the road. This superb 17th century house is the most interesting in the district and looks entirely lost in this rural setting. Its south front is a remarkably intricate four bayed labyrinth of mullioned windows. The monks of Furness Abbey had a grange here, and farm life still thrives.

Before Friars Head, however, on a bend after the bridge, double back to the right on a firm wall-side track. This runs on beneath a wood covering an old quarry to demise at a wall corner. Cross to the wall corner opposite, and rise outside the wooded confines of the beck to run along to Brockabank. Before reaching it, look back to see the splendid old limekiln at the edge of the wood: up behind is another old quarry. *Take a stile by the gate in the very corner, from where a green way passes along the front of the house.* With its mullioned windows and exquisite location, this is a beautiful, isolated old place, a gem dating back to the 17th century. Down below, the wooded environs of the beck further contribute to the charms of this lovely corner.

The drive is joined and leads quickly down to the arch of Brockabank Bridge. Up to the left through the trees is an extensive old quarry face, with another limekiln just below. *Part way up the other side, on a slight bend, take a stile and slant up the field brow on the left to the top corner of a plantation. Cross the paddock alongside Eshton Grange to emerge back onto the road.*

Cross to a stile opposite and make for a stile in the fence ahead, then cross the field to another stile. Across the next narrow field a kissing-gate leads into the woods, and a good path heads through trees, passing a large remote dwelling before emerging into a large field. The delightful parkland hereabouts is part of the former park of Eshton Hall. *Descend straight down to an iron stile and maintain the same course to a stile to emerge onto a road on the edge of the village.*

Either double back to a junction and then turn right as far as Ray Bridge on the canal, or simply keep straight along the direct road into Gargrave. Either leads to a short canal towpath walk (right) back to the canal crossing near the start of the walk. Ray Bridge marks the northernmost point of the Leeds-Liverpool Canal.

Friars Head

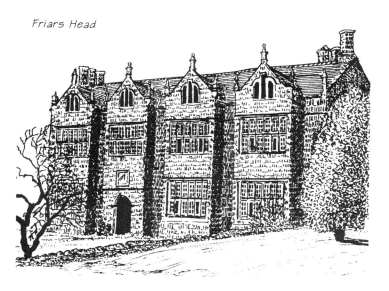

18

EAST MARTON

START Gargrave   Grid ref. SD 931541

DISTANCE 7 miles

ORDNANCE SURVEY MAPS
1:50,000
Landranger 103 - Blackburn & Burnley
1:25,000
Pathfinder 661 - Skipton & Hellifield *or*
Outdoor Leisure 10 - Yorkshire Dales South (1995 edition)

ACCESS Start from the bridge in the village centre. There are two car parks just around the back from the cafe opposite. Gargrave is served by the Skipton-Settle bus, and also by train.

This rural amble is dominated by a towpath trod that exhibits a remarkable variety of interest. For a note on Gargrave please refer to page 68.

☐ **Cross the bridge over the Aire in the village centre and turn immediately right on the made path upstream. This runs past several houses and alongside a contained beck, to leave the riverside green at a corner and emerge onto a street. Turn left to join Marton Road. Go right a short way, then go left along an enclosed driveway to Scaleber Farm. This runs on for some time, largely between hedgerows, and bridging high above the railway line.** At this point the route of the Pennine Way joins in, and remains our way to the canal at East Marton.

After climbing to a cattle-grid, the drive is left by bearing gently away up the field. A fainter branch from the drive is joined to point the way up to an old stake. Here on the brow we have a fair prospect ahead, to Pendle Hill dominating the scene. Back over our left shoulder are the heights of Flasby Fell, backed by the higher

Cracoe Fell with its monument prominent. To the right meanwhile, are the Malhamdale heights leading the eye up to the very beginnings of the Aire.

Continue on to a kissing-gate, then head away with the fence to a stile at the end. Bear left over the field to the next corner stile, then head away with the fence again. From the next stile drop left to a stile by a gate over the tiny sike of Crickle Beck. Now follow it away alongside the fence to the right, to reach a bridge and ford. Don't cross, but from the stile here continue downstream, alongside the parallel fence on the left. When the fence parts company slant back to the beck, and a little further we reach a plank footbridge to cross it. Bear left up the field to reach a stile in the far bottom corner. Here a rough lane is joined. *For a short-cut, turn right here until picking up the main route on the canal bank.*

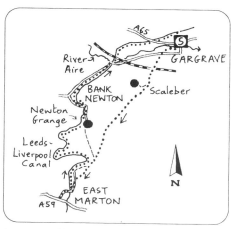

Turn left along the lane and at the first opportunity, within 200 yards, take a stile on the left. This short section short-cuts a large bend in the lane. Cross straight over the field to a stile on the left of the wood ahead, from where a short-lived walled way rises alongside the trees. A novel stile at the top sees us back out. Continue up alongside the wood, enclosing a quarry abandoned long ago. When the wood turns sharp right, bear away from it to locate a stile at the far side, just short of another small wood. This admits to the now surfaced lane. Follow it left past further recolonised quarries, quickly reaching Williamson Bridge on the canal at East Marton.

There are always plenty of boats moored here, while just ahead, the A59 is seen crossing the canal by the well known double-arched bridge. The reason for this strange arrangement is simply the busy nature of the road: the older, lower arch has long been superceded by the need for the sturdier, higher one.

Gargrave Bridge, on the river Aire

Our return route takes to the towpath here, but the few attractions of the hamlet may first merit attention. Continuing straight over the bridge, some attractive housing is passed - that to the right sporting mullioned windows, including some arched-headed, and alongside is a licensed tearooms. Just up the lane, alongside the main road, is the ever popular Cross Keys *serving good ale and meals, and a small green. The parish church is somewhat out of the way, on the other side of the A59.*

Returning to the canal, the route description comes to an end. Though the walk is not yet halfway through, all that remains is to follow the waterway back to Gargrave. *Its various meanderings ensure that this is a longer return, especially in the early stages where a glance at the map confirms the canal's attempts to hold its contour result in a right old weaving about. This section has a curiously remote feeling to it. Ahead, Flasby Fell forms a colourful backdrop, flanked by Cracoe Fell to one side and Embsay Crag on the other.*

Approaching Bank Newton, the old lane is rejoined for a short section before it crosses the canal. Here double back under the road bridge to regain the towpath, just short of the first of Bank Newton's locks. *There follows a splendid string of such locks, seven in all. This section is full of interest, and summer weekends are likely to see much activity by the boating fraternity.*

The moorings follow the locks, beyond which another short road section is forced until the next bridge. Doubling back underneath Priest Holme Bridge, the bank offers immediate further interest, first in an aqueduct above the river Aire, then straight under the railway, with its viaduct over the river visible just downstream. The final section sees Gargrave's scattered locks begin, the third being alongside the popular Anchor Inn. All day refreshments and a large outdoor area and playground may well divert attention. Happily the canal then takes us under the main road, to conclude round the back of the village. Across the canal stands the substantial Gargrave House.

At the road bridge at Higherland Lock (milestone: Liverpool 93, Leeds 34¼), finally abandon the towpath and turn down the lane to re-enter the village, alongside the main car park.

Double-arched bridge, East Marton
(carrying the A59 over the canal)

19

FLASBY FELL

START Skipton   Grid ref. SD 990518

FINISH Rylstone   Grid ref. SD 969586

DISTANCE 7½ miles

ORDNANCE SURVEY MAPS
1:50,000
Landranger 103 - Blackburn & Burnley
1:25,000
Outdoor Leisure 10 - Yorkshire Dales South **or**
Pathfinder 661 - Skipton & Hellifield

ACCESS Start from the parish church at the head of the High
Street. There are several large car parks in the town. Skipton
is on the Airedale rail line from Leeds/Bradford, and is served
by bus from all surrounding towns. Rylstone is on the B6265,
served by Grassington-Skipton buses.

*Skipton is derived from 'sheep-town', for wool has played an
important role for many centuries. This capital of Craven has much
to offer, and a first-time visitor will find insufficient time to explore
its attractions. Skipton occupies a strategic location in the Aire
Gap, owing, to this day, as much allegiance to East Lancashire as
the West Riding of Yorkshire. This low-level route through the
Pennines has been used both for trade and military purposes, and
in more recent centuries has been exploited by both canal and rail.*

*The broad High Street, with its spacious setts up either side, is a
lively scene on market days (Monday, Wednesday, Friday, Satur-
day). A variety of stalls squeeze cheek by jowl in front of the shops.
Pride of place goes to the parish church at the head of the street.
14th century features include part of the tower. Damaged during
the Civil War, the church, like the castle, was repaired by Lady
Anne Clifford. Of note are the rood screen of 1533, the great oak*

beams of the medieval roof, and the Clifford tombs. Around the altar are those of Henry, 1st Earl of Cumberland (1542), and his wife Margaret, each superbly depicted on brass; Francis (1589), infant son of George, the Third Earl; and the tomb of the Third Earl himself (1605), richly decorated with Clifford armorial bearings.

Mention of the Cliffords leads to the finest building in Skipton, its well-preserved castle. Adjacent to the church, it hides its glories, round a corner from the head of the High Street. Its first greeting is an enormous early 14th century gatehouse with rounded towers: it was restored by the indomitable Lady Anne, and the motto 'Desormais' - henceforth - is her work. Inside is a spacious green and the castle proper. While the newer section of the castle is a family home, the western half is open to visitors. A visit is certainly justified - one particular feature of interest is the cramped conduit court, in the centre of which grows a renowned yew tree.

The castle dates from Norman times, being founded by the de Romilles, coming into the Cliffords' possession in 1309, when it was largely rebuilt. What is on show is for the most part either early 14th century, or later additions by Henry, 1st Earl of Cumberland and by Lady Anne over a century later. For 3½ centuries it was the home of the powerful Cliffords. Henry the 10th (Shepherd) Lord spent his youth in anonymity in the company of monks and

The Gatehouse, Skipton Castle

shepherds before being returned when Henry VII came to the throne after Bosworth in 1485; George, 13th Lord and 3rd Earl, was a sea captain who helped overcome the Armada; while his remarkable daughter Anne, last of the Cliffords, still journeyed between her various castles - including Brougham and Appleby, in Westmorland - at a ripe old age to restore and maintain them.

Skipton and the Cliffords featured in both the Wars of the Roses and the Civil War. Though it stands proudly in Yorkshire, its border location saw allegiance to the red rose county in the first conflict: Thomas, 8th Lord, paid with his life at St. Albans in 1455. In the latter they fared little better, for this Royalist stronghold was taken and held by Cavaliers. Who'd have the Cliffords on their side?!

A short excursion around the back of the castle, by crossing Mill Bridge over Eller Beck, leads by way of three parallel watercourses - the beck, the Springs Branch of the canal - down which quarried stone was brought - and a mill-cut, to view the impregnable northern face of the castle, a sight witnessed by few visitors. From this central location Skipton Woods, a recent acquisition by the Woodland Trust, extends up behind the town. Also worth visiting is the Craven Museum in the Town Hall, while the Leeds-Liverpool Canal glides through the heart of town. Colourful boats can be hired to explore into both Lancashire and Yorkshire from this self-proclaimed 'Gateway to the Dales'.

☐ **From the small roundabout outside the parish church, take the Grassington road past the** Castle Inn, **and over a bridge.** Beneath are Eller Beck and the Springs Branch of the Leeds-Liverpool Canal. **Turn immediately right along a minor road, Chapel Hill, which climbs steeply to end at a gate and stile.** Thus we have made an exceptionally rapid escape from the heart of the town to open country. **Climb straight up the field to a stile at the very top.** Close by is the barely discernible site of a battery, a defensive position where a cannon was mounted in the days of the Civil War. As a lookout post it was well chosen, with extensive views over the town and the Aire Gap. **From here continue in the same direction towards the by-pass, which is gained by crossing a farm lane parallel with it.** The much needed Skipton by-pass was completed in 1984. **Cross with care and from a stile on the other side head directly away again, to a stile which admits to Skipton golf course.**

Continue straight across, passing a short section of wall to arrive at the wall ahead, with a small length protruding our way. Take the stile on the left and follow the fence away, crossing one final stile

before accompanying a left-hand fence down onto Brackenley Lane. Turn left up the lane to its junction with the Skipton-Grassington road, and cross to a stile directly opposite. *The* Craven Heifer *inn is just along to the left, an early possible refreshment halt.* **Aim for a stile at the far side of the field, then head away from it alongside a fence which soon falls into disrepair: continue up the gentle slope to reach a gate onto a lane just above the** Tarn House Hotel.

Turn right along the lane and at the third sharp bend, take a gate on the left to follow a wide, gently rising track. After two more gates open country is entered: when the accompanying wall breaks off left, leave the track by bearing off right. On climbing the slope a faint path material-ises, and improves as the top of Sharp Haw is neared and the going steepens a little. An old iron stile fitted in the wall across the top admits to the Ord-nance column on Sharp Haw's airy summit.

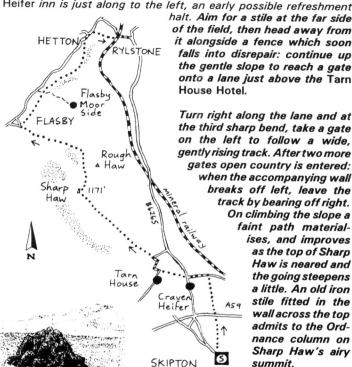

Rough Haw, to Cracoe Fell

Sharp Haw is the highest point of Flasby Fell, the large triangle of upland between Skipton, Gargrave and Rylstone. Ably supported by Rough Haw, it is a familiar sight to travellers approaching Skipton up the Aire Valley, and the pairing have always been the author's 'gateway' to the Dales. Though close neighbours, these colourful tops are anything but twins: their titles are apt enough description. To the north of Rough Haw are two rounded, lesser heights.

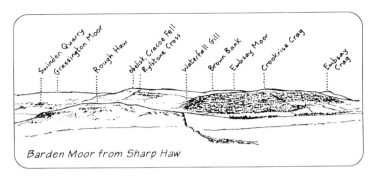

Barden Moor from Sharp Haw

Neighbouring Rough Haw sits across the depression to the north, and this is the line of our next objective. Follow the path along the short ridge for a few yards, then it drops to the right to a gateway in the wall there. The path heads straight down the slope and across the depression to a gate and stile. Directly in front are the short, steep slopes of Rough Haw. The main path, however, heads along to the left. The short scramble onto Rough Haw (no right of way) involves climbing the steep path directly ahead, to pass through an outcrop of rocks before levelling out to reach the cairn.

On the main path a fork is quickly reached: while the more obvious branch descends to the left towards the top corner of a wood, the right of way forges straight on, a clear path through the bracken flanks of Rough Haw. Further on it swings down to the left itself, out of the bracken now and with a wall just beyond. Descend the near side of the wall, once again swinging round to the left near a corner to drop down alongside Septeria Gill to a gate in the very bottom corner, where the direct path is met. Continue along the edge of the field to another gate, from where an enclosed track winds down to the yard of Flasby Hall Farm. Flasby is a tiny settlement consisting of a few scattered houses and farms: it was originally founded by the Danes. A little further downstream stands Flasby Hall.

Over the bridge take a gate on the right, and cross a couple of paddocks to the beckside. Follow it upstream, and at a barn head up the centre of the field on a pronounced embankment, now high above the beck. This runs to the far side, where a fence is joined to lead back down to the beck. Beyond a gate is a gap-stile, just past which a farm drive is crossed to another such stile, and a vague path runs upstream to a ladder-stile defended by a marsh.

80

Head up the slope behind, and then on through a couple of stiles. The way ahead is clear to and beyond the next stile, after which the faint path slants down, yet again, to the beck at the far end.

Ignore the footbridge in favour of our current bank, and continue on a path upstream. The houses of Hetton now appear ahead, and the path, beyond one more stile, slants up to the left, forsaking the beck to cross to a stile to the left of a hut. One last field is crossed to a stile onto the road on the edge of Hetton. Turn right into the village. Hetton is an attractive village largely free of tourist crowds, though the Angel Inn attracts folk from far and wide to dine.

The final leg leaves by an inviting green way down the side of a barn, at the major road junction by a small green before reaching the pub. This zigzags down to the beck again, though at the first bend stiles indicate a footpath short-cutting a small corner. The beck is crossed in style by a hoary old slab bridge. Supported by two lesser acolytes, its hollowed centre suggests it has seen the passage of many generations of feet and hooves. *A walled snicket heads up the other side, joining a drive to emerge alongside the railway onto the road.* The railway is a mineral line serving the massive Swinden limestone quarry beyond Cracoe. It originally ran to Threshfield, for Grassington, but lost its passenger service decades ago. *Turn right, under the rail bridge to enter Rylstone.*

Rylstone is the tiniest of villages, but has much of interest. Alongside the main road is the attractive pond, fringed in April by daffodils, and formerly the village green. Near the church was the home of the Norton family, who took part in 1536 in the Pilgrimage of Grace, and three years later the Rising of the North. Their unfortunate story is recounted by Wordsworth in his White Doe of Rylstone.

St. Peter's, Rylstone

RYLSTONE EDGES

START Rylstone   Grid ref. SD 969586

DISTANCE 6 miles

ORDNANCE SURVEY MAPS
1:50,000
Landranger 103 - Blackburn & Burnley
1:25,000
Outdoor Leisure 10 - Yorkshire Dales South *or*
Pathfinder 661 - Skipton & Hellifield

ACCESS Start from the pond alongside the main road. There
is parking alongside, and also just along the road at a lay-by.
Rylstone is served by Skipton-Grassington buses.

• *Note before starting: this walk takes in part of Barden Moor access
area, which may be closed at certain times. Please refer to page 7.*

*Rylstone is the tiniest of villages, but there is much of interest here.
Alongside the main road is the attractive pond, fringed in April by
daffodils, and once the village green. Near the church was the
home of the Norton family, who took part in 1536 in the Pilgrimage
of Grace, and three years later the Rising of the North. Their
unfortunate story is recounted by Wordsworth in his* White Doe of
Rylstone. *There is an old milestone hidden on the junction across
from the pond. From the outset both Rylstone Cross and the Cracoe
obelisk sit waiting high above.*

☐ *From the pond, cross the road with care and head up the lane
opposite. Passing the Manor House on the right, it leads to the
church. Just beyond, turn right along a rough track to the far corner
of the field. Here take a stile, and follow the wall away, now on the
other side of the track. Both cross and obelisk are still prominent
on the moorland skyline. On passing through a tiny wood at the*

end, an open field is entered. Cross straight over, right of a pocket of trees, to a stile in the wall opposite. Ahead is a walled lane, which is joined by way of a stile just ahead. Advance only a hundred yards along it, then take a gate on the left. This is an entry point to the access area.

A splendid track heads through the reedy pasture, climbing steeply past an island-plantation and up to a gate. Here the access area proper is entered. Continue up the track, now through dense bracken cloaking innumerable sunken ways. As the track starts to level out, a green way heads off to the left. This quickly points to a thinner path, which slants clearly up out of the bracken to slant beneath the tumble of rocks above. It soon reaches a stile at a wall-corner. Over the other side of the wall is the great heathery expanse of the heart of the high moor. For now follow the wall away, enjoying sweeping views to quickly reach Rylstone Cross.

Rylstone Cross stands atop a high, natural gritstone base. It was erected to celebrate the Paris treaty of 1813, and is a prominent

landmark from the Skipton-Grassington road. The view includes Rylstone church tower, Hetton, Rye Loaf Hill, Kirkby Fell, Ingleborough, Fountains Fell, the Birks Fell ridge, Yockenthwaite Moor, Buckden Pike, and Great Whernside. In the winter of 1992/1993 the old stone shaft with its wooden arms succumbed to severe gales, and was only re-instated - with the assistance of a helicopter, initially - in the spring of 1995.

The Cracoe Fell obelisk is the next objective, and there are two ways of reaching it. The traditional walk is along the moor-side of the wall. Cross the ladder-stile and head off along a well worn path, which undulates (passing an 'R' (Rylstone)/'C' (Cracoe) boundary stone) **but gradually climbs the extra 350ft to reach another stile giving access to the obelisk.** More intrepid walkers will remain on the virtually pathless 'edge' side of the wall. This enjoys superior views, in place of the equally grand moorland atmosphere. Of the *several groups of rocks hogging the edge, the second one demands a modest scramble to descend through, or an alternative descent to pass beneath all the rocks. Some of these outcrops - notably those supporting the cross, and the next group beyond - offer superb gritstone climbs, including Yorkshire classics such as 'President's Slab' and 'Dental Slab'. In all there are well over a hundred named routes on these crags, which are sufficiently high and remote to attract only those climbers still able to fellwalk.*

If remaining on the edge path (you must do one or the other from the start, the wall is not intended to be climbed), then eventually, beyond a monster rock, the wall curves around to a ladder-stile at a junction. Cross it and make the short climb to the obelisk, largely on a splendid green hollowed way.

The obelisk on Cracoe Fell is even more prominent a landmark than Rylstone Cross. It is Cracoe's memorial to its war dead, and looking out over such a green and pleasant land (quarries excluded) it is a poignant reminder of what our forebears - many who would barely have been out of their own village until then - sacrificed for us to enjoy today. The solid structure is made of the same rock on which it is safely perched, and not surprisingly it commands a glorious view. Its moor-edge location ensures that the distant Dales mountains featured from Rylstone Cross are ably complemented by a richer collection of village clusters such as Hetton, Threshfield and Grassington.

From the obelisk, next objective is the head of Fell Lane climbing out of Cracoe. It will be seen just to the right of the village, and just to the right of a stream at the foot of the moor. While one could make a direct descent, engaging, for a while, a sunken way directly beneath us, there is a far more useful old way to be found. Head along the slope from the obelisk, in line with the wall over to the right, a faint trod forming: this meets the sunken way starting to go down beneath the obelisk. Cross straight over to find another winding down, on a bend. Turn down it past a basic stone shelter, the way immediately unmistakable now as it slants down the fell.

Like those met on the ascent, these innumerable braided ways are old sledgates, worn deep by the passage of sledges loaded with quarried stone, and long since grassed over. **This great groove absorbs several other such tracks, leaving the rougher slopes then eventually doubling back to falter in the reedy ground before the bottom wall.**

The intake gate is just along to the left, defended by sheep pens. The lane is a splendid green way itself in its first half, before the addition of a farm track makes it more standard. At a cottage it becomes surfaced, and just before reaching the main road, there is a chance to avoid it. Turn left along a narrow lane, right at the end, then sharp left again as it runs behind the Devonshire Arms.

The little settlement of Cracoe marks the barely discernible watershed between Airedale and Wharfedale. Its long, low white-walled inn has a good few years' history behind it, and like several others in the district it bears the arms of the family on whose moor we have just been tramping. There is also a very popular cafe next door.

At a junction at the end keep straight on, with the charming company of a little stream for a while before leaving the village behind. On reaching the main road, don't join it but take a gate on the left, from where the walled trackway of historic Chapel Lane climbs away. This quickly levels out and runs a very pleasant course back towards Rylstone. Towards the end, note the base of a former wayside cross. *By the trees at the end, don't turn right to the road, but take the gate ahead. Advance along the wall-side to Manor House Farm on the right.* Note, on the left, the grassed over banks still supporting the ancient fish-ponds. *From a gate at the end the lane-head at the start of the walk is rejoined. Follow the lane back past the church, finishing with a cautious crossing of the road.*

Rylstone Cross

85

CROOKRISE CRAG

START Embsay   Grid ref. SD 998544

DISTANCE 6 miles

ORDNANCE SURVEY MAPS
1:50,000
Landranger 103 - Blackburn & Burnley
            104 - Leeds, Bradford & Harrogate
1:25,000
Outdoor Leisure 10 - Yorkshire Dales South

ACCESS Start from Embsay Moor Reservoir, reached by Pasture Road off Elm Tree Square at the top of the village. There is a water authority car park. Embsay is served by bus from Skipton.

• *Note before starting: this walk takes in part of Barden Moor access area, which may be closed at certain times. Please refer to page 7.*

☐ *Embsay Moor Reservoir has a fine setting under Embsay Crag and the moor itself. Its facilities are shared by Craven Sailing Club and Skipton Angling Association.* **From the car park, head along the stony track outside the reservoir, past the sailing club to the far end. Here its confining walls break away and a stile gives access to the open moor. Turn left onto a path beginning an immediate climb, soon accompanying the wall on the left. Remaining near the wall, the path further improves and passes through characterful boulder scenery before levelling out. Soon a stile in the wall is reached: use it to attain the top of the cliffs of Crookrise, a breathtaking moment.**

The panorama revealed stretches across the whole of Craven, from the Aire Valley to the South Pennine moors and round to West Craven and the familiar outline of Pendle Hill. Beyond are the Bowland moors, and then the Malhamdale hills of Kirkby Fell and company intervene. Flasby Fell's tops are directly in front, while the higher reaches of the Dales fill in the rest of the scene to the north.

86

Now confined in the narrow space between the steep drop and the wall, continue northward, straight towards the white trig. point which soon comes into sight. At 1361 ft, this is Crookrise Crag Top. The vast expanse of heather-clad upland known as Barden Moor comes to an abrupt halt at many places around its rim, but nowhere as dramatic as Crookrise, where a long line of crags fall steeply to an un-natural green carpet. In between are a tumble of millstone grit boulders, and this whole scene forms a splendid sight for travellers on the road between Skipton and Rylstone. The crags are substantial enough to offer a varied range of challenges for rock climbers.

After surveying the extensive panorama described opposite, take another stile to return to the moorland side of the wall, and continue northward. On reaching Hellifield Crags (the second and much more substantial rock outcrops met) a steep drop to Waterfall Gill

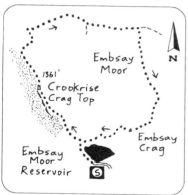

is encountered. *This is largely avoided as a sketchy path slopes across to the right, past the lower boulders of Hellifield Crags to meet the beck without too much height loss.* Just before reaching the beck a fine waterfall should be seen from up above. *Once across, accompany the crumbling wall as it climbs the bank. The gradient soon eases and the wall eventually leads to a gateway where the Rylstone-Bolton Abbey track passes through.*

Our route takes advantage of this way, and turns to the right along it. This historic route was immortalised by Wordsworth in his poem The White Doe of Rylstone. The story of the ill-fated Nortons of Rylstone tells off a widow undertaking the trek over the moor to visit her husband's grave at Bolton Priory: the pet deer that accompanied her continued the journeys even after her death. Followed onto the heart of the moor, the distinct path has recently seen much restoration at a notoriously boggy section by the laying of a more durable surface. *This remains our way for almost a mile and a half.* During this time we absorb a more solid shooters' track coming up from a pair of thatched cabins, and continue to stride out in grand style.

At a guidepost and small cairn, a thin trod strikes through a gap in the heather, bound for Embsay. This is our way. It runs faintly across the moor, with Embsay Crag gaining in prominence ahead. An old track comes in from a small quarry back up to the right, and the way runs on to drop towards a gate off the moor. Instead, bear right, joining a path from the gate which leaves the wall to cross towards the striking profile of Embsay Crag. As the ground steepens the path keeps above the increasing tumble of rocks to rise pleasantly to the highest point, a location which is not in doubt.

Embsay Crag is a notable landmark in the Skipton area, jutting as it does from the vast expanse of moorland. A rich cloak of bracken covers the lower slopes, while a delectable carpet of heather crowns the top. The 'crag' is actually a tumble of large boulders heaped together in wonderful chaos on the southern slopes of the hill. This is gritstone country at its best, and the highest rocks are the perfect location for a long lazy break on a hot summer's day, with the reservoir shimmering far below our airy vantage point.

The main path can clearly be seen descending the steepest section directly below, and is well blazed through the bracken beyond. A much friendlier way down, however, is to follow a very sketchy path along the brink of the rocks across to the right: this descends in similar fashion to our route of ascent, and after exchanging the heather for bracken another path is met. Turn left along it to join up with the main path down from the crag. This path leads unerringly down to a footbridge by the head of the reservoir, having earlier passed a left fork which takes in the old quarry. From the footbridge avoid boggy ground by heading half-right to join a wide track, which followed to the left leads to the stile back off the moor.

Crookrise Crag, looking over
Flasby Fell to the Malham hills

22

EMBSAY MOOR

START Embsay   Grid ref. SE 009538

DISTANCE 7 miles

ORDNANCE SURVEY MAPS
1:50,000
Landranger 103 - Blackburn & Burnley
            104 - Leeds, Bradford & Harrogate
1:25,000
Outdoor Leisure 10 - Yorkshire Dales South

ACCESS Start from Elm Tree Square at the top of the village. There is a car park a few yards further along Main Street. Embsay is served by bus from Skipton.

• *Note before starting: this walk takes in part of Barden Moor access area, which may be closed at certain times. Please refer to page 7.*

Partly inside the National Park boundary, Embsay is a thriving and sizeable village, perfectly sandwiched between Skipton town and the open moors. The Hall has 1652 and 1665 datestones. It was here the Augustinians began work before opting for the Wharfe's banks to found Bolton Priory. Today Embsay is the home of a preserved railway, and a most enjoyable hour or two can be spent on a good honest steam train. There are also two pubs, the Cavendish *and the* Elm Tree.

☐ **Leave the village by the stile at the back of the car park, and bear left to a stile at the top corner of the field. The slender path slants up again, then crosses the fields behind the school and houses.** *Up to the right the heather topped, bracken flanks of Embsay Crag beckon, with Crookrise Crag set back to its left. Both these eminences are visited on WALK 21.* **In a longer field, approaching a lone house on the right, a stile will be found down** *in the corner. This admits to a lane. Opposite is the attractive millpond which is popular with ducks and swans. The attractive house overlooking it, just along to the left, bears a 1665 datestone.*

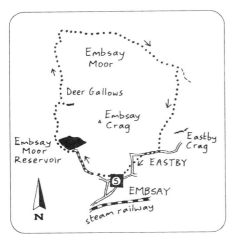

Turn right along the lane which rises to the grassy dam of Embsay Moor Reservoir. A shame the waterworks buildings couldn't be better masked, but the bracken clad moorland flanks set the pulse racing. Bear left up to the corner of the reservoir, and head along the stony track alongside. Try to detect the location of a raking trackway on the slope ahead: though initially less obvious when on top of it, it should soon nevertheless be underfoot. When the wall parts company, take a stile in the fence to gain the foot of the open moor.

A level green track heads away. Within yards, after crossing a marshy streamlet, turn unconvincingly up through the bracken, with marsh on your left. Crossing a drainage ditch, slant a little more and a clearer path forms. This quickly becomes a very distinct green way, raking up through bracken alongside a sunken way. The surroundings are truly magnificent: Embsay Crag across to the right, and a bird's-eye view of the shimmering reservoir. Look back over Skipton to the Aire Valley, which is backed by the Pennine watershed, re-forming after the major interruption of the Aire Gap.

Embsay Crag
from the reservoir

90

The track makes a broad sweep, becoming less clear as a thin path opts to go straight up. Heather begins to dominate now, while the rocks of Deer Gallows make an inviting landmark over to the right. *Without realising it, we are, effortlessly, already virtually level with the top of Embsay Crag. Almost on the brow now, at a small cairn, Deer Gallows is just five minutes across to the right. The tantalising path becomes a little clearer, then fades again. On the open top, a trod is met at right angles in the moor grass.* One could keep straight on over this, but would sacrifice Deer Gallows.

Go right through a few reeds to a line of grouse butts. At butt no. 6, advance along a clear trod to have a look at Deer Gallows. This is a really superb spot, and popular with climbers who make the effort to forage across the moor. The main cliff face is archetypal millstone grit, tilted gently back and riven by great rounded gashes. Its crest makes a fine place for a sojourn. Facing it, yards distant across a green floor, is the added attraction of a rock tower, composed of exactly the same layout, block upon block.

From the crest of the main stones, return to butt no. 6 and head back along the clear trod to the start of the marshy tract, then turn up through the grass on the right. Almost at once our faint green track espies a more solid shooters' track, and quickly runs on to become it.

Deer Gallows

A thatched shooters' cabin at Hutchen Gill Head, looking over Lower Barden Reservoir to Simon's Seat

Very quickly the true brow of East Harts Hill is gained, with a magnificent prospect of the interior of the moor. Cracoe Fell's obelisk sits on the skyline ahead. In late summer, these rolling heather seas are positively outstanding. *Keep straight on, soon dropping to Waterfall Gill and rising to a pair of thatched shooters' cabins.* These come as quite a surprise, traditionally constructed of local stone with a delightful thatch-like topping. Even the shape is rather unique. *Keep straight up to meet the 'White Doe' bridleway coming in.* This historic route was immortalised by Wordsworth in his poem The White Doe of Rylstone. The story of the ill-fated Nortons of Rylstone tells off a widow undertaking the trek over the moor to visit her husband's grave at Bolton Priory: the pet deer that accompanied her continued the journeys even after her death. *Turn along to the right, enjoying long strides on a grand track.*

At a guidepost and a small cairn, a thin trod breaks away through a gap in the heather, bound for Embsay: ignore this and keep straight on. A new view is revealed as Simon's Seat and Barden Fell appear across the delectable valley of the Wharfe. *Just yards beyond, a track heads off left to Upper Barden Reservoir.* Lower Barden Reservoir comes into the scene soon, and more of Wharfedale is revealed. *Avoiding numerous such distractions, we descend with this glorious prospect, with a growing feeling that this is to be a descent into Wharfedale.*

At a crossroads with an inviting green path to the left, take a slender trod to the right. It runs clearly on to the breached dam of an old reservoir at Hutchen Gill Head, then straight on a short lived trough to a shooters' cabin. Just beyond is another, but turn up to the right before it. This rising track quickly forks - keep left to run along to the first of a row of butts. Follow these on a faint green pathway to their demise. Over to the right, Embsay Crag is seen at its finest angle. Ahead is Skipton Moor, high above a quarry, with the Rombalds Moor skyline back to its left. With green fields ahead, it becomes clear we are running out of moor!

Approaching the final butt, a thin trod bears gently left to a stile adjacent to Eastby Gate. Pass through some pens and down the wall-side track. A nice moment is gained above the side gill ahead, with Embsay Crag's profile reaching an exalted status. **The track descends above it to become deeply ensconced in a hollowed, leafy way, before emerging into a yard at Eastby and down onto the road.** Eastby is a tiny farming village strung along the lane from Embsay over the moor to Barden. It does however boast a pub, the Masons Arms, and is the terminus of the Embsay bus from Skipton.

Turn right, leaving the village and then leaving the road at a stile on the left. There is a certain quaintness to the tarmac strip of a path, not more than a foot wide as it runs through the fields to Embsay Church. At the road, follow it left past the church, and take a stile on the right. Aim across to the next stile, from where an enclosed path heads away. Emerging, Embsay's car park is just below, with the day's first stile leading into it.

At the millponds, Embsay

93

SOME USEFUL ADDRESSES

Ramblers' Association   1/5 Wandsworth Road
London SW8 2XX   Tel. 0171-582 6878

Yorkshire Dales National Park Information Services
Colvend, Hebden Road, Grassington, Skipton, N. Yorks. BD23 5LB
Tel. 01756-752748

Malham National Park Centre - Tel. 01729-830363

Tourist Information

9 Sheep Street **Skipton**   Tel. 01756-792809

Town Hall **Settle**   Tel. 01729-825192

Bolton Abbey Estate office -Tel. 01756-710227

Yorkshire Dales Society
Otley Civic Centre, Cross Green, Otley, W. Yorks. LS21 1HD
Tel. 01943-607868

The National Trust   Regional Office
Goddards, 27 Tadcaster Rd, York YO2 2QG Tel. 01904-702021

Friends of National Parks
Council for National Parks, Freepost, London SW11 1BR

The Woodland Trust
Freepost, Grantham, Lincolnshire NG31 6BR Tel. 01476-591691

Dales Connections - *comprehensive transport timetables*
Elmtree Press & Distribution, The Elms, Exelby, Bedale,
North Yorkshire DL8 2HD (send 50p for p + p)

British Rail, Leeds-Skipton-Carlisle/Morecambe lines
Tel. 0113-244 8133

LOG OF THE WALKS

WALK	DATE	NOTES
1		
2		
3		
4		
5		
6		
7		
8		
9		
10		
11		
12		
13		
14		
15		
16		
17		
18		
19		
20		
21		
22		

INDEX

Principal features: walk number refers